HOUSEPLANTS

MARY LAMBERT

TREASURE PRESS

First published in Great Britain in 1983 by Octopus Books Limited

This edition published in 1986 by
Treasure Press
59 Grosvenor Street
London W1

ISBN 1 85051 147 0

Printed in Hong Kong

Contents

The publishers wish to thank the following organizations and individuals for their kind permission to reproduce the photographs in this book.

Michael Boys/Octopus 63; John Moss/ Octopus 26, 27, 59; Octopus Library 31, 51, 55; Roger Phillips/Octopus 35, 47, 70, 95; Harry Smith Horticultural Photographic Collection 43, 71.

Illustrations by Ed Roberts 5, 36, 37, 40, 44, 45, 53, 56, 60, 61, 64, 69, 88, 89.

CARING FOR YOUR PLANTS

Collecting plants to decorate and add beauty to your home can become a very interesting hobby. You can have all the usual gardening excitements and benefits without having to worry about the climate! It doesn't matter whether you live in a cramped flat in the city or a spacious house in the country, you can select plants to suit your particular tastes and location. As all plants differ with regard to the conditions they like, plan your displays accordingly. For instance, some hate draughts so would not like being near a badly fitting window; some love humidity and would flourish in either a bathroom or kitchen. Even dark corners that never get much light can be enhanced, with an ivy for example.

When arranging plant displays, it is best to group together those which like similar conditions. They can then create their own micro climate, giving each other humidity – and should flourish accordingly. Trailing plants in hanging baskets can be very effective – a *tradescantia* is one of the easiest to cultivate. Other plants like *rhoicissus* can be trained to climb along bookcases or shelving units.

CHOOSING PLANTS
Before you go out to buy your plants think carefully about the type of conditions you can offer. If your home is very cold, for example, there is no point buying a tropical plant that needs continuous warmth.

The houseplant sections later in the book have been classified with stars for easy reference. One star means the plant is easy to grow and ideal for the beginner; two stars means the plant needs more attention and should only be added to your collection when you have gained some knowledge of plants; three stars means the plant is difficult to grow, often needing high temperatures and high humidity.

When you have decided where you are going to put the plant and consequently what conditions it will live in you can begin the enjoyable search for a suitable one. Always consult the plant care card that is sold with most plants, as this will tell you the basic requirements. If you decide on a flowering plant to add beauty and colour to your home, always buy a healthy looking plant with maybe two or three flowers out but plenty of green buds – avoid brown buds as they are signs of an unhealthy plant. A plant with plenty of healthy buds may flower continuously for up to two months. When buying foliage plants, avoid those with broken or injured stems, limp leaves, leaves which have turned yellow or those that are brown at the edges or have brown spots; these are all signs of neglect or disease. Similarly if you see insects on the leaves or stems, don't buy the plant.

THE PLANT'S ENVIRONMENT When you have chosen your houseplant or plants, having first considered the conditions it or they are going to live in, you can put them in their allotted places.

Temperature It comes as a surprise to many beginners with houseplants that temperature is not as important as light and the right watering. Many plants will grow quite happily at a minimum temperature of about 10°C (50°F).

However, very few plants will survive frost and care must be taken when choosing plants for a room where the temperature will fall below 7°C (45°F). At that particular temperature many plants will live only as long as they are kept dry, though some – like the cacti – positively enjoy it. If your home is centrally heated keep a careful watch on your plants, especially when the heating is up high, as they will probably need extra humidity – spraying them regularly will help.

Light All houseplants need light as they all carry out photosynthesis – the process by which they make their own food supplies. The ones which survive in more shaded conditions are just more adaptable. Plants with variegated or brightly coloured leaves almost always require good light; otherwise their colour will lose its brightness. Be careful, too, with plants you keep on a window sill. Although they will certainly have adequate light they might get scorched by too much sun – windows actually intensify the heat rays. Plants with fleshy leaves like the *peperomia* are particularly vulnerable. Situating plants a distance from the window helps.

WATERING Plants, like humans, consist of a large percentage of water, in their case about 90%. They give off water vapour by transpiration through their leaves and this is replaced by water being drawn up through the plant's roots. Water also dissolves the nutrients the plants need to grow and survive. It is therefore essential to follow your plant care instructions and give it the specified amount of water. Too little will cause wilting of the stems and leaves, and the leaves will go yellow; too much produces the same problems.

Lukewarm tap water should be poured into the plant from the top in an even flow until it fills the space between the compost and the rim of the pot. To avoid root-rot, remove excess water from the pot holder.

There are several methods you can use for holiday watering. One is to place the plants on a water absorbent plastic matting and filter water gradually through a tube from a higher container onto the mat. The roots then absorb the moisture as required. If you have only a few plants they can be watered well, then wrapped in transparent polythene bags; this will enable them to create their own small climate.

HUMIDITY AND FEEDING The right humidity – the amount of moisture in the air – is

Water plants from above filling up to the rim.

Dry plants can be immersed until air bubbles appear.

Mist a plant regularly and stand on shingle in water for lots of extra humidity.

extremely important for plants, especially when so many homes have central heating.

So the right balance is essential. Shallow containers of water placed near plants provide a suitable surface from which water can evaporate. Regular spraying or misting is also a good idea, especially during the summer.

Plants need the right amount of nutrients to give them the energy for healthy growth. The most important of these are: nitrogen, potassium and phosphorous. Small amounts of other 'trace' elements are also used by the plant and include magnesium, calcium and iron. A correctly-balanced compost will usually provide all the necessary nutrients, but during the plant's growing periods these may be used up too quickly and will need to be replaced with liquid fertilizers.

GROOMING Pay particular attention to the appearance of your plants to keep them looking healthy and attractive.

Leaves (except hairy ones) should be kept clean and free of harmful dust and grit. Glossy-leaved plants like the rubber plant *(Ficus elastica)* can be cleaned with a sponge moistened in water, and their glossy state maintained by using the leaf shine preparation available in flower shops.

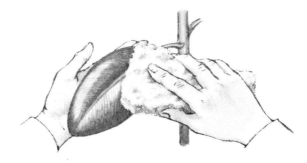

A rubber plant can be gently cleaned with a sponge.

Plants' leaves can be gently washed in water.

CONTAINERS

Today, most plants are sold in plastic pots which are lighter to carry than the original clay ones and virtually unbreakable. But unlike clay pots, plastic ones are not porous and careful watering is needed to avoid making the plants waterlogged. Clay pots are still available and some people find them more attractive to use.

Many other types of container can be used for plants. For example, you can have window boxes of wood or polystyrene in which a pleasing variety of plants can be displayed on a window ledge indoors just as well as out. But if you do use this type of large container indoors, don't be over-generous with your watering sessions – or untold damage to decorations could result! In any event, wooden containers should always be treated with a proprietary preservative against the deteriorating effect of dampness. Outdoors, window boxes should always be firmly anchored to the sill.

Plant pots can be bought in a pleasing variety of shapes and materials – particularly attractive are the patterned ceramic ones either bought for a song while on holiday in Spain, Italy or France, or at rather more expense in the gardening department of large stores and at garden centres. Craft centres, too, are a rich source of unusual containers, including one-off designs that may cost a little more but give you the satisfaction of having something unique.

Urn shapes make particularly elegant containers for the more upright plants and are also ideal for trailers. And what could be more stylish than the traditional Victorian

jardiniere? Or, if one of these is a little beyond your pocket, there are some very presentable modern versions available now.

Of course, not all containers need be very grand. In fact, some plants seem to lend themseves happily to something on a humble scale – such as a small but prettily enamelled casserole or saucepan, now past its prime.

Whatever your choice, remember to provide good drainage or you will very soon have to deal with rotting roots and a sadly wilting plant.

COMPOST To ensure a healthy, thriving plant you must use
the correct compost. It is through the compost that the plant absorbs water, oxygen and all the essential nutrients for normal growth. The precise ideal mixture of compost varies for different plants but normally a well-balanced type is widely acceptable. This contains a mixture of loam, granulated peat, coarse river sand, fertilizer and chalk, specially balanced to allow good drainage for the plant, aeration of the compost, a supply of food for three months and an adequate amount of water for the roots. It is also fairly heavy, so firmly anchor the plant in its container.

There are also modern light composts available which do not contain soil. They consist of peat and sand in the ratio of 3:1, with some additional fertilizer. However, they are not suitable for some larger plants which need heavier compost.

POTTING AND REPOTTING

How often you need to repot varies from plant to plant, but the first thing you have to learn is to recognize the signs that warn you the plant needs repotting or a larger pot. Fortunately, these signs are usually pretty obvious: pale straggly leaves, normal watering is not sufficient and the roots are coming out of the drainage holes. Newly-bought plants might have *some* protruding roots but this will have originated from the way they have been grown; obviously, they will not need repotting.

Some plants which grow very quickly may need repotting twice or three times a year, but generally they might need it just once a year, and some are happier to remain in the same pots, a little overcrowded.

When to pot The most suitable time for repotting is normally early spring at the start of the growing season, although plants can be repotted up to the summer months. Autumn and winter are not suitable for repotting as the plant slowly stops producing new growth and the roots do not take much food or water out of the compost.

To transfer a plant into new rich compost during this time, when the roots could not absorb the extra water or the nutrients would cause the compost to go stale, could introduce bacteria and be harmful to the plant.

How to pot The first thing to decide is what new size of pot you need for your plant. An accurate guideline to follow is that a space of 1.5-2.5cm (½-1in) should be left between the root ball and the side of the pot. If using a clay pot, put a few broken pieces of clay in the bottom to improve drainage and aeration and put a thin layer of compost on top.

Remove the plant from its old pot by turning it upside down, and, with one hand round the stem of the plant to protect it, give the side of the pot a sharp tap with the back of a hand-trowel to loosen the plant which should then slide out easily – complete with soil ball. Carefully loosen the soil ball and remove any straggly or completely brown roots. Put the plant in its new pot and fill the sides of the pot with compost, leaving a space of 1.5-4cm (½-1½in) between the surface of the soil and top of the pot for watering. Gently press down with your fingers but not your thumbs which will make the soil too firmly packed. Soil-less composts should be only lightly firmed. Shake the pot carefully to level the soil, water and then place in a warm, slightly shaded position away from draughts and direct sunlight.

Occasionally, you need to repot a plant with new compost rather than transfer it to a larger pot. Gently ease out the plant, remove the old compost from the root ball and untangle the roots; add the new compost until the pot is filled to the correct depth, firming as you proceed.

Prickly cacti are obviously difficult to take out but they can be removed with a pair of tongs, a cardboard collar or a strong pair of leather gloves.

Protruding roots mean the plant needs repotting

Carefully take the plant out of the pot, supporting the foliage

Leave 1.5-2.5cm (½-1in) between plant and pot

Leave 1.5-4cm (½-1½in) between soil and the top

Even the soil and give adequate water

Remove cacti with cardboard collar

PROPAGATION

SEEDS This is the easiest way to propagate new plants. Sow in a pot or box of moist seeding compost with broken crocks at the bottom. Cover the pots with a plastic bag or group them together under glass. Keep in a warm place and remove the condensation that collects every day. When the seeds germinate, place them in full light and, when the seedlings become crowded, plant in individual pots.

Place seeds in moist compost

LEAF CUTTINGS

Propagation by this method is particularly suitable for plants like gloxinias and begonias. Take a mature leaf with a 4cm (1½in) stem from an existing plant, dip stem in hormone rooting powder, and insert in a pot containing an equal mixture of peat and sand. Water well, cover with a polythene bag supported on sticks and keep warm.

New plants at each bud

OFFSETS Some plants multiply by sending out from the parent plant small runners with baby plants. It is therefore very easy to propagate them. Place the mature plant in a tray full of potting compost, securing the runners to the compost with hair pins or paperclips.

Alternatively, put the baby plants into individual pots where they will take root; then sever from parent plant.

The parent plant sends out runners

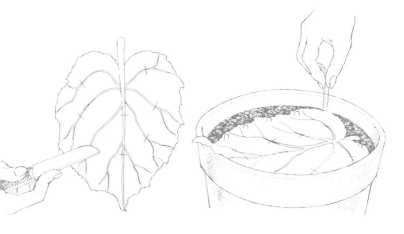

Cut the leaf veins

Secure leaf with hairpins

VEIN CUTTING *Begonia rex*

is an ideal plant for this method of propagation. Take a large leaf from the mature plant and make cuts through the larger veins on the underside. Place and pin the leaf, right side up, on a pot full of damp sand. The pot should be covered with a plastic bag to help propagation and kept warm. In a short time, plants will grow in the vein cuts.

Plantlets appear in the cuts

STEM CUTTINGS

From a plant like the chrysanthemum, cut a side shoot about 10cm (4in) long; cut the section just below a bud and remove the bottom leaves. Put about a third of the cutting in a good potting mixture and place in a warm place. Hardwood cuttings grow in the same way but a 15cm (6in) cutting needs to be taken as they take longer to root.

Another method is to take a stem with no leaves and split it into pieces, each with a bud. Cut the top and bottom of the bud and remove a bit of bark opposite the bud. Put this stem on potting compost, keep warm and soon small plants will grow.

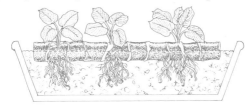

Plants form at the base of the stalk

AIR LAYERING This is a particularly ideal method to get new plants from the rubber plant *(Ficus elastica)*, monstera, camellia and hibiscus, especially when they have grown too high. Make an upwards cut in the stem near the top of the plant and liberally coat the area with hormone rooting powder.

Securely attach a piece of polythene with string beneath the cut and fill with dampened sphagnum moss, then seal the top. Roots from the main plant will start to grow through the moss in about three weeks.

Carefully water the plant and when the boots are firmly established, remove the plastic covering and neatly cut the plant off below the new root ball. Put the new plant in a separate pot.

If a new plant has been made because the old one has become unattractive and straggly, do not hesitate to discard the parent plant once you are certain that the new one is well established.

PESTS AND DISEASES

Some of the most common plant pests are spider mites, whitefly, scale insects, mealy bugs and aphids (greenfly). Spider mites, pale yellow or red in colour, often attack plants, especially when there is nice hot, dry air. If your plant has been infested, spray thoroughly with Malathion solution, repeat again twice with ten-day intervals until the plant is cured.

If the plant's leaves have turned a greyish colour and are curled, it is probably under attack from whitefly. Remove the badly infested parts and spray the plant several times at intervals of three to four days with Bioresmethrin which kills the larvae; the adults also soon die off. Brown scale insects, which attach themselves to the back of the leaves and cause brown or yellow spots, can be gently knocked off. After thorough cleaning spray the plant with Malathion.

Mealy bugs, dark-grey in colour, feed off the stems of plants and cause severe damage. Spraying with Malathion will cure mild attacks. Aphids attack the tips of new shoots and the underside of leaves. The plant makes poor growth and becomes distorted, and the leaves curl and turn yellow. Aphids also encourage the growth of the black fungus, sooty mould. They can be successfully sprayed with Derris or Malthion and the mould washed off with a mild detergent. Rinse with water afterwards.

Fungus diseases rarely seem to attack houseplants but the most common are mildew and grey mould. Mildew, causes a white, patchy powder on the tops of the leaves. Remove the affected parts and spray with a fungicide or dust with sulphur. Grey mould thrives under moist, cool temperatures. Brown patches appear on the leaves and then a fluffy grey fur. Cut off the affected parts and treat with Benomyl once a week for three weeks.

A virus attack makes the plant stunted with blotchy and yellow leaves. There is no cure; the plant must be destroyed.

Always take due care when using insecticides. Read the manufacturer's instructions **before** you use them, and store any leftover out of reach of children.

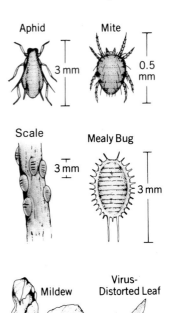

Aphid — 3 mm

Mite — 0.5 mm

Scale — 3 mm

Mealy Bug — 3 mm

Mildew

Virus-Distorted Leaf

PROBLEM CHART

DAMAGE	CAUSES AND TREATMENT
Bottom leaves turn yellow and drop.	Too much water in compost. Remove from container for a day to dry out. Do not water for several days.
Bottom leaves turn yellow but remain on plant.	A cold spell or temperature drop. Check temperature.
Yellow mottling with rings or streaks, slow growth and stunting.	A virus infection carried by such insects as greenfly (see page 15).
Yellow specks and web on leaves or stems.	Red spider mite (see page 15).
Leaves lose variegation and become green.	More light is needed if all leaves have become green. If only one branch, remove affected shoots.
Edges and tips of leaves become brown.	The air is too dry. May have too much lime in water or compost. Increase humidity and remove from any draughts.
Hard brown or pale yellow spots on leaves.	Scale insects (see page 15).
Powdery white patches on plant.	Powdery mildew (see page 15).
Little white furry spots on stems and leaf joints.	Mealy bugs (see page 15).
Brown and yellow marks plus furry, grey patches.	Grey mould (see page 15).

DAMAGE	CAUSES AND TREATMENT
Greyish leaves, new growth is weak, falling leaves.	Red spider mite (see page 15).
Curling and distorted leaves, sometimes turn yellow.	Check for greenfly or scale insects (see page 15).
Leaves have sticky patches.	Honeydew from greenfly or whitefly (see page 15).
Falling leaves, bud drop.	Cold or draughts, wrong watering, too little sun. Check care procedures.
Plant fails to flower.	Lack of food and light. Give potash feed and more humidity.
Beige coloured, wavy lines and blisters on leaves.	Leaf miner is probably responsible. Remove affected leaves.
Fleshy leaves which turn brown at soil level.	Too much water; cut off infected part and spray with benomyl.
Sticky patches on leaves.	Scale insects (see page 15), greenfly or whitefly.
Hyacinth florets brown or flower spike stunted.	Not enough water when the bulbs were developing roots.
Brown rotting of stems at soil level.	Cold combines with overwatering.
Plant looks greyish and 'tired', spots growing, has a rather dry appearance.	Possibly root aphis or root mealybug. Turn plant out of pot for a day; do not water.

DECORATING WITH PLANTS

WINDOW BOXES, BALCONIES AND PATIOS An ideal way to brighten up a bare window sill, balcony or maybe a neglected patio is to add a few plants.

The choice of plants for your 'garden' is infinite; obviously plants which enjoy a lot of sun will thrive. Trailers like *tradescantia* and *F. Pumila* (*Ficus* family) are useful to cover containers or to feature in hanging baskets. Wallflowers, daffodils and hyacinths are just some of the spring flowers which can be particularly attractive; marigolds, dwarf antirrhinums and pinks are glorious in summer; bedding dahlias and chrysanthemums help to extend the summer glow into autumn and snowdrops and Christmas roses brighten up the winter.

Window boxes are still one of the most popular ways of growing plants outside, especially with people living in towns who do not have gardens. The boxes are particularly suitable for seasonal flowers and can be used for cropping vegetables. Standard potting composts should be used.

Window boxes should be made of wood or asbestos and fastened to the sill.

Even restricted areas like the front entrance to a flat can be made more attractive by training clematis along the railings and filling urns with flowering plants.

When planning a balcony garden and deciding how many plants to have, bear in mind the not inconsiderable weight of the containers and compost you are going to use, plus your own and other people's weights, or you could over-load it. For this reason, soil-less composts and light-weight containers are always a good idea. Expanded polystyrene containers are light and they retain warmth. It is up to you to decide whether to use urns, tubs, large pots or less conventional containers. Making sure that water drains properly from containers is also important, because heavy rain can soon drench plants. Prevent this by using broken clay pieces, shingle or gravel.

HANGING BASKETS Open-wire baskets are still very

popular, and using them is a simple matter. Line the basket with sphagnum moss or osmunda fibre and fill to about 4-5cm (1½-2in) from the top with peaty soil.

Plant the sides of the basket as well as the top as you go along. The basket must be thoroughly watered regularly, preferably every day when the plants are flourishing. They should be fed weekly from July until autumn.

To prepare for planting

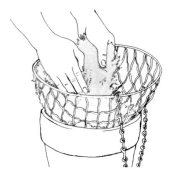

line with sphagnum moss

Then fill with rich soil mix

Basket ready for planting

NOVEL CONTAINERS

There are often times when you are looking for a different sort of container to show off a particular plant in an unusual manner.

Old wine bottles can be simply adapted to house semi-woody plants like dwarf fuchsias, pelargoniums, plectranthus and coleus. The best sort of bottles are those with thick rims and domed bases. Make a 2.5cm (1in) diameter hole in the centre of the dome with a diamond or similar instrument. Thread a thick piece of wire right through the bottle, hooking one end firmly over the base. Enough wire should be left to run through to the top and be shaped into a hook for hanging.

Turn the bottle upside-down and half fill it with equal amounts of sand and sifted loam. Put two or three cuttings with roots into the base opening. Turn the bottle the right way up so that the soil drops and secures the plants. Water the plants through the neck opening and hang the bottle up in a light, window area. At first the plants hang down but they soon grow upwards and in time the complete bottle is covered.

Parsley is a herb which is always in demand in the kitchen and an ideal and pretty way to grow it is to plant it in a

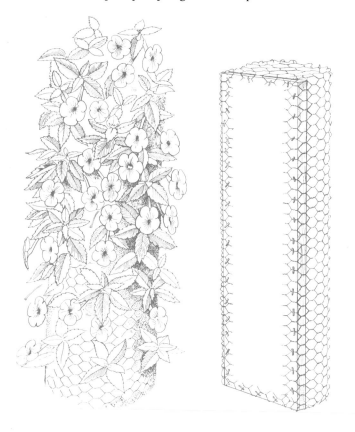

terracotta parsley pot. This is shaped like a chimney and has many 1.5cm (½in) holes all round the sides. Parsley pots are usually sold with a large saucer to hold the water.

Plant the seeds in a seed tray or a container of soil and leave until the seedlings become well established. Then fill the parsley pot with potting mixture or coarse sand, peat and sifted loam in equal measures. Transfer the seedlings carefully, planting some through each hole and some in the top. Put in a place with plenty of light, water regularly and the plants will quickly grow. You can use an old casserole dish to make a small herb garden which can be kept nearby on the window-sill for easy picking.

To make an unusual log garden, take a plank of wood, cover it with an arch made out of sphagnum moss, secured with wire netting as shown below. (Use staples to fix the wire at the back of the plank to keep the moss in position.) Place small plants like achimenes, small bromeliads and dwarf begonias in the front. Attach a hook to the top so you can hang up the log garden. Water thoroughly by soaking in warm water for 10 to 20 minutes.

If you have an old glass fish bowl lying around you can make another interesting type of container. Make up a pan of peat or soil and put the glass bowl over it. African violets flourish when grown in this way.

If you are lucky enough to happen upon one of those Victorian chimney-pots relegated to a builder's skip – or see one for sale in the high street antique shop, snap it up. They make perfect containers for trailing plants and the castellated ones look charming on a patio.

SITUATING PLANTS WELL
Buying plants is reasonably easy compared with the task of placing them in the right situation to achieve maximum effect.

Obviously, one good situation for plants is on a window-sill or in a window recess, but you must choose your plants carefully. Take care also if there is a radiator just below the window as this creates a hot, dry atmosphere which attracts pests such as the red spider mite. A shelf just above a radiator is also a bad location – for the same reason. If space by the window is rather restricted it is worth considering hanging pots. Normal pot holders can be adapted by drilling three evenly spaced holes just below the rim; three slender chains or nylon string can then be threaded through.

When the window ledge is narrow, trough-style containers are a good idea, as several can be butted end to end for a full display. For a south-facing window the trough could include sansevieria, impatiens, tulips and cyclamens.

Placing plants at different levels in a room can create unusual and attractive effects, especially when the plants high up are trailers such as the spider plant.

Kitchens can also house plants successfully. Some jungle plants such as *gynura* and *codiaeus* love the warm humidity.

A good plant mixture for south-facing windows

ROOM DIVIDERS

Potted plants can be an interesting way of dividing a room into, say, a living-dining area.

Square or oblong containers are best for room dividers as they can be placed end-to-end, or back-to-back as required. Some are fitted with capillary watering systems which cut down on regular watering.

If big plants are being used, the containers must be large enough to accommodate the sizes of pots required. A liner of plastic or metal to collect moisture and some gravel for the pots to stand on should also be included. The container will also need to be fitted with a support for the plants to climb on. A simple trellis is one easy answer. Another method is to screw a 5x2cm (2x1in) slat into the ceiling above the container and fit eyelet screws into the slat. It is then a straightforward matter to fasten thick nylon string from the eyelets in the slat to eyelets screwed into either side of the container, thereby forming an open tent shape up which the plants can climb naturally or be trained to climb.

Two of the best climbing plants to grow in poor light conditions are the grape ivy *(Rhoicissus chomboidea)* and *Philodendron scandens*. A plant well known for its fast growth is the vine, *Tetrastigma voinieriana*.

A trellis provides a frame for plants to climb

FOLIAGE PLANTS

Houseplant care symbols:
*easy **medium ***difficult

These are some of the most popular of the houseplants
available. There are numerous varieties, all infinitely different,
to be purchased. Whether you choose plants with variegated
leaves, large glossy leaves or maybe long, spiky ones they can
be used to decorate, generally enhance and personalize your
home.

AGLAONEMA**
(Chinese evergreen)
These plants originate in South-east Asia and need warm
temperatures with high humidity. They grow straight up and
have large variegated leaves which can grow to about 23cm
(9in) in length and about 7.5-10cm (3-4in) in width,
depending on the particular species.

Aglaonema is featured on the left

Position They succeed well in light or shaded places with no draughts, but variegation is better in the light. They do not like gas fumes.
Temperature A minimum temperature of about 10°C (50°F) is recommended.
Watering Water about twice a week in summer and once in winter.
Feeding Feed every two weeks during the summer months.
Pests and disease These plants can be prone to mealy bugs which attack the closely-grouped leaves.

ARAUCARIA EXCELSA*
(Norfolk Island Pine)
This pine originates from Norfolk Island in the Pacific. It is very easy to grow and has short evergreen leaves which resemble needles. Clustered together on the stalk they resemble fronds. The plant seems like a fern with a trunk rather than the miniature tree it actually is.

With care it will grow to a height of 1-2m (3-6ft). The plant is happiest in a reasonably warm atmosphere with normal humidity; a dry atmosphere and poor ventilation can cause leaf drop.
Position The plant prefers good light or just a little shade.
Temperature A minimum temperature of about 7°C (45°F) is necessary.
Watering Water twice a week in summer but literally just moisten the soil in winter.
Feeding Feed every two weeks during the summer months with only half of the recommended dose.
Pests and disease Can be infested by mealy bug and greenfly.

Begonia rex is featured in the centre

ASPIDISTRA ELATIOR*
(Asparagus fern)
This particular plant was extremely popular during the
Victorian era and is becoming so again today. The plant
originates from the lower slopes of the Himalayas in China
and was first cultivated in 1822. It can grow to 45cm (1½ft) in
height and the leaves grow in clusters on short stalks.

One of the reasons for the aspidistra's former popularity is
that it is very hardy and survives most conditions; even
over-watering.
Position The plant prefers good light but survives very well in
shaded areas.
Temperature Minimum temperature should be about 4°C
(40°F). *A.e. variegata* requires more light to maintain its white
stripes.
Watering Water twice a week in summer and once a week in
winter. If the plant is overwatered, brown spots will appear at
the roots.
Feeding Feed once a month in summer.
Pests and disease Can be troubled by mealy bugs, red spider
mites and scale insects.

BEGONIA REX***
This plant, unlike its other flowering species, is grown solely
for its colourful, unusually shaped foliage. On top of the rather
delicate, crinkled green leaves can be found a lovely blend of
colours: pink, red, silver, cream, grey, lavender and maroon.

Plants can reach 60cm (2ft) in height and 60cm (2ft) in
diameter but are normally grown as much smaller plants.

Aspidistra elatior

Position Strong sunlight should be avoided but the plant likes a position in good light with a humid atmosphere and no draughts.
Temperature Minimum temperature about 15°C (60°F).
Watering Water twice a week in summer and every ten days in winter.
Feeding The plant should be fed every two weeks in summer.
Pests and disease Can be attacked by red spider mites, fungus and mould.

CALATHEA***
(Peacock plant)
These are beautiful plants, as their popular name suggests, with leaves in many shades of green and brown. *C. makoyana*, with its wonderfully patterned leaves, is one of the most striking varieties. *C. zebrina* has velvety leaves of light and dark green. *C. insignis* has foliage that is bushier and smaller but equally impressive. Temperature for these plants is extremely important and the minimum must be maintained.
Position A shaded position is preferred with a moist atmosphere.
Temperature A minimum temperature of 13°-16°C (55°-61°F) must be carefully maintained.
Watering Follow care instructions carefully and ideally use rainwater as tap water can leave white marks on the leaves.
Feeding Feed as instructed on the care label.

Begonia rex

28

CHLOROPHYTUM COMOSUM*
(Spider plant)

The spider plant is extremely easy to cultivate and could really be called the modern equivalent of the aspidistra. New plantlets grow at the end of long stems radiating from the parent plant, and soon develop roots – even in mid-air! This species with its variegated, long, spiky leaves is the most commonly found. It can grow to about 37cm (15in) tall and 45cm (18in) wide. The plant will become much more variegated if kept near a window in good light. If placed in a dull corner it will become a rather pale green all over.

Position A location with good light – but not direct sunlight – is ideal, but it can survive well in slightly shaded areas.

Temperature The minimum temperature should not fall below 7°-13°C (45°-55°F).

Watering Water two to three times a week in summer and once a week in winter.

Feeding Feed every two weeks in summer.

Pest and disease Can be attacked by the red spider mite and greenfly.

CISSUS ANTARTICA**
(Kangaroo vine)

An attractive climbing plant which, as its name suggests, originated in Australia. It is an evergreen with glossy, serrated green leaves which look like large beech leaves. It can grow to around 15-30cm (6-12in) a year and needs a support around which it curls.

The Kangaroo vine grows particularly well in places that

Chlorophytum comosum

have a bit of shade like halls, or north facing window sills or landings. A dry atmosphere can cause the leaves to curl up; so give them an occasional spray to counteract this.

Position Cool, shaded places with some humidity.
Temperature A minimum temperature of 13°C (55°F) is recommended.
Watering Water about twice a week in summer and about every two weeks in winter.
Feeding Feed every two weeks in summer.
Pests and disease Red spider mites and greenfly can be a problem.

CITRUS MITIS**
(Miniature orange tree)
This is a delightful little tree which is particularly prized. A lot of people try to grow citrus plants from pips but they can get too large and be erratic in their production of fruit – the orange tree is much more reliable.

The trees originate in the Philippines and are quite hardy but prefer plenty of sun, heat and humidity in summer. They are bushy evergreens and reach about 30-45cm (1-1½ft) in height. White blossoms are produced in the spring and at intervals up to the autumn. The fruits are orange and about the size of a walnut – 3.5cm (1½in) across.

Position Sunny, warm window ledges are ideal.
Temperature The minimum temperature allowable for this plant is 10°C (50°F).
Watering The compost should be fairly moist in summer; water occasionally but keep fairly dry in winter.
Feeding Feed twice a week during the summer months.

CODIAEUM VARIEGATUM PICTUM***
(Croton, Joseph's coat)
Strikingly-coloured leaves are the outstanding feature of this evergreen plant which comes from Malaya. Delicate veining in the leaves emphasises the red, yellow, orange, brown and green colours.

The plants in pots are normally 45-60cm (1½-2ft) high and need to be kept where there is steady warmth and humidity. If there is a sudden temperature drop the leaves are likely to fall off.

Position Natural light, but not direct sunlight, is preferred. Sudden temperature drops and draughts should be avoided.
Temperature A minimum temperature of 15°C (60°F) is needed.
Watering Water twice or three times a week in summer but only once a week in winter.
Feeding Feed every two weeks in summer.
Pests and disease The plant can be infested by red spider mites, mealy bugs and scale insects.

COLEUS**
(Flame nettle)

These plants are renowned for their rainbow leaves with unusual colour combinations of red, bronze, yellow and white. They are ideal plants for the summer and autumn and like plenty of water and light. However, they are not worth keeping throughout the winter months as they become faded and very weak and sickly. Cuttings can be taken though for new plants for the following spring.

Position Coleus like good light but not direct sunlight.
Temperature Minimum temperature required is about 13°C (55°F).
Watering Water freely during the summer months.
Feeding Follow care instructions; feed generously during the summer months.
Pests and disease Watch out for grey mould and greenfly.

CORDYLINE TERMINALIS**
(Cabbage palm)

Beautifully-coloured leaves stand out on this plant which comes from Eastern Asia, New Zealand and Australia. The leaves are long and shaped like spears and are red, green or cream in colour. The plant can grow to about 60-90cm (2-3ft) and the leaves can be as long as 30cm (12in). *C. indivisa* is hardier with narrow, bronze-red-green leaves on a stem maybe 90cm (3ft) tall.

Position Likes an area with good light but not hot sun.
Temperature Minimum temperature of not lower than 13°C (55°F) is needed.
Watering Once or twice a week during the summer months; about every 7-10 days during the winter.
Feeding Feed every two weeks in summer.
Pests and disease Can be weakened by red spider mites.

CUSSONIA SPICATA*

A handsome tree which will grow quickly, even when the roots are confined in a large pot. The leaves are glossy and dark green with purple undersides. Their shape is palmate and, on mature plants, deeply divided. Do not buy this plant unless there is plenty of room for it to grow. It is necessary to repot it every year and to keep it in a loam-based soil. Obviously, a clay pot is required, rather than a light plastic one. New plants can be raised from seed relatively easily.

Position Keep in a light position, but not direct sunlight.
Temperature Minimum temperature required is about 7°C (44°F).
Watering Water freely during the summer months.
Feeding Feed generously during the summer.
Pest and diseases Can be attacked by red spider mites.

CYPERUS DIFFUSUS**
(Umbrella plant)

A very aptly named plant with narrow leaves which emerge from the top of the stem and then bend over slightly, resembling the spokes of an umbrella. The plant can grow to a height of about 90cm (3ft) or more in height. In spring and summer small groups of brown and white flowers are produced from the tops of the umbrellas. *C. Papyrus* is the Egyptian reed and can reach heights of 3m (10ft).

Position A good light is preferred but not hot sun.

Temperature A minimum temperature of 15°C (60°F) is recommended.

Watering Water three times a week throughout the year and always keep standing in a little water.

Feeding Feed every two weeks during the growing season.

Pests and disease Can be attacked by greenfly and whitefly.

Cyperus

DIEFFENBACHIA**
(Dumb cane, Leopard lily, Mother-in-law plant)
This versatile plant, which originates from Central and South America, has more than 55 varieties, many of which have truly outstanding foliage – but only a few can be grown other than in greenhouse conditions. If there is a drop in the temperature, the leaves will drop too! However, it is well worth cultivating the few varieties suited to a home environment. The handsome green foliage bears striking variegations in cream and white, and the leaves can grow up to 23cm (9in) in length.

D. Exotica (Leopard lily) is a particularly attractive species, with ivory markings on the leaves and a vivid-green mid-rib. In the right conditions its leaves can grow to exceed 30cm (1ft). If, however, you prefer a more compact plant, 'Camilla' – which has an overall white tinge – is a good choice. With this and other compact forms, sideshoots are readily produced from the base.

On a cautionary note, if you wish to propagate dieffenbachias by removing some of these young growths and repotting them, take care not to get any of the sap on your fingers. If you do, wash your hands immediately because the sap can be highly poisonous. The common name Dumb Cane came about because it is said that if the sap gets on to your tongue it is capable of rendering you speechless for some time. Certainly, the plant should be grown well out of the reach of young children and family pets.

Position Keep away from draughts; prefers a slightly shaded position.

Temperature Minimum temperature of about 10°C (50°F) is normal.

Watering Water about twice a week in summer and once a week in winter but do not drench.

Feeding Feed once a month in summer.

Pests and disease Mealy bugs and red spider mites can be a problem.

DRACAENA*
(Dragon tree)
The natural habitat of Dracaenas is the tropical regions of India and Africa. They are grown for their foliage which varies a great deal in shape and colour with the different species.

The plants all need warmth and humidity. *Dracaena sanderiana* is a tall, slender plant. Its leaves are grey-green in colour with creamy-white stripes. *Dracaena godseffiana* is a very different plant – it is a low growing, bushy plant with dark green leaves flecked with cream. *Dracaena fragrans* has much longer, broader leaves and in its homeland can grow to 6m (20ft). In a pot the leaves grow to about 10cm (4in) wide and have a central yellow band.

Position Plenty of light is ideal but should be kept away from direct sunlight.
Temperature Minimum winter temperature of about 7°C (45°F).
Watering Water about twice a week in summer but only once in winter.
Feeding Should be fed once a month in summer.
Pests and disease Red spider mites, fungus and mealy bugs can be troublesome.

EUONYMUS JAPONICUS*
(Spindle tree)
Although the Spindle tree was first grown in Japan it is also grown in parts of Britain such as Devon, Dorset and Wiltshire. This very compact species is ideal for bottle gardens where it really flourishes in the moist, mini climate. The leaves are shaped like spoons and have a slightly serrated edge. The 'Aurea' variety has a bigger leaf which is a lovely golden colour. The 'Micro- phyllus' variety is smaller. If a plant grows too quickly in the bottle garden and is cramping the others it can be pruned back with nail scissors.
Position Good light is needed but not direct sunlight as the glass will intensify it.
Temperature A minimum temperature of about 7-10°C (45-50°F) is recommended.
Watering Must not be overwatered. Water only when the compost is dry.
Feeding Only moderate feeding is necessary.

Dieffenbachia

FATSIA JAPONICA*
(False castor oil plant, Fig leaf palm)
Fatsia japoncia has been a household favourite for a while
now. It comes from Japan and Taiwan. It grows to a height of
about 2.4m (8ft) and has large glossy leaves which are palmate
shaped and have about seven or nine lobes. They should be
gently cleaned at regular intervals to keep them glossy. It is a
very adaptable plant but does prefer cool temperatures in
winter.
Position A position of good light is ideal.
Temperature A minimum of about 13°C (55°F) is
recommended.
Watering The soil should always be kept moist in summer; but
just keep from drying out during winter.
Feeding Feed once a week from the months of April to September
and not at all during the winter.
Pests and disease Virtually untroubled but can be attacked by
grey mould if overwatered.

FICUS ELASTICA ROBUSTA*
(Rubber plant)
This is one of the most popular houseplants today and must
surely rival the favourite of the Victorian era, the aspidistra, for
the number of plants sold. An easy plant to cultivate it is one
which can really look attractive in your home. It survives
extremely well even in low temperatures or where there are oil
or gas fumes. Special care should be taken with the leaves
which are dark green and leathery. They should be gently
sponged clean with tepid water to keep them shiny. The
rubber plant will grow to a height of approximately
1.2m (4ft).
Position Prefers good light and dislikes draughts.
Temperature The plant is best suited to a minimum
temperature of about 7-18°C (45-64°F).
Feeding Feed every two weeks during the summer months and
not at all during the winter.
Pests and disease Scale insects, mealy bugs and red spider
mites can infest the plant.

FITTONIA***
(Snakeskin plant)
The natural habitat of fittonias is the rain forests of Peru. They
are named after the Fitton sisters who, in 1850, published a
book called *Conversations on Botany*. Small in size the plants
have oval leaves with white, delicate veins. They prefer humid,
constantly warm atmospheres with no variations in
temperature. The variety *Fittonia argyroneura* is a creeping
plant and *F. verschaffeltii* has darker green leaves with red and

cream markings. The newly-introduced 'snakeskin' variety is a miniature form of *F. argyroneura* and is hardier and easier to grow.

Position A shaded position is required with a humid atmosphere and constant heat. Avoid draughts and direct sunlight.

Temperature The minimum temperature required is about 16°C (61°F).

Watering Water two or three times a week in summer but only once a week in winter.

Feeding Feed every two weeks in summer with half the normal dose.

Pests and disease The plant can be troubled by greenfly and grey mould.

Ficus elastica robusta

HEDERA HELIX**
(Ivy)

These pretty small-leaved ivies are very easy to cultivate if they are treated well and grown in the right conditions – they will not tolerate a hot, dry atmosphere. There are several variegated varieties which can add contrast and interest to your plant arrangements. As natural climbers they can be trained to twine round trellis work, hang from macramé baskets or even climb banisters. Two particularly good buys are 'Little Diamond', which has grey-green leaves featuring a white margin, and *sagittaefolia* which has leaves like arrows.

Position They like a good light and a humid atmosphere; they dislike central heating.

Temperature 7°C (45°F) is the minimum temperature needed.

Watering Once or twice a week during the summer months but only once a week during the winter.

Feeding Feed every two weeks in summer.

Pests and disease Can be prey to greenfly, scale insects, red spider mites and moulds.

Hedera helix

HEPTAPLEURUM ARBORICOLA*
(Green rays)

A native of South-east Asia, this plant with its palmate leaves of deep green can either be grown effectively on a single stem or it can be made more bush-like by removing the top of the plant. Leaves can be rapidly lost if there are drastic changes in temperature or in the amount of water it is given. Keep the soil just moist throughout the year. The plant can grow to about 1.8m (6ft) in height, depending on its containers.

Position Will grow well in a slightly shaded position but prefers more light in the winter.

Temperature A minimum temperature of 15°C (60°F) is normal.

Watering Keep moist throughout the year but don't overwater.

Feeding Follow care instructions carefully.

MARANTA**
(Prayer plant)

A lovely foliage plant which gets its common name from the way its leaves fold up at night and look like praying plants.

Most of the marantas come from Brazil, where they can be found growing in clearings in the tropical forests. They are evergreen and spread by means of short runners.

Maranta leuconeura 'Kerchoveana' has leaves which are pale grey-green with brown markings. *M. leuconeura* 'Massangeana' has smaller leaves which are more olive-green in colour with white markings. All plants thrive in a humid atmosphere with a lot of warmth.

Position Marantas like good light but not direct sunlight.

Temperature A minimum temperature of 15°C (60°F) is necessary.

Watering Water two to three times a week in summer but only once a week in winter.

Feeding Feed half the recommended dose every two weeks in the summer.

Pests and disease Can be attacked by red spider mites.

Maranta

MONSTERA DELICIOSA*
(Swiss cheese plant, Mexican bread plant)

Monsteras, now one of the most popular houseplants in this country, originates from Mexico. They grow best supported by some sort of stake so that they can climb freely. The leaves are a glossy green, can be very large and have long slashes. In the right conditions plants can grow as tall as 3m (10ft) and the leaves can be as long as 1m (3¼ft). They like a fair amount of warmth all the year round and do well in centrally heated homes providing there is enough humidity.

All monsteras produce aerial roots from their stems and if these are directed into moist moss sticks or water the plant will benefit. The leaves of monsteras should be regularly sponged or cleaned with a proprietary leaf cleaner to help keep their natural gloss.

Position Good, natural light is preferred but not direct sunlight; tolerates some shade but leaves will be smaller.
Temperature Monsteras can cope with a minimum temperature of about 10°C (50°F).
Watering Water about once a week in summer and about every two weeks in winter.
Feeding Feed every two weeks during the summer months.
Pests and disease The pest most likely to cause problems is the red spider mite.

PEPEROMIA**
(Desert privet)

Numerous varieties are available. Their growth is compact and bushy and they originate from the tropical forests of South America and the West Indies.

One of the most popular peperomias is *Peperomia caperata* which has distinctive leaves with light and dark green shading. *P. magnoliaefolia* has rounded, fleshy leaves which, when variegated, are cream and green. The leaves of some peperomias have an almost quilted appearance.

A humid atmosphere with steady warm temperatures is preferred by all the varieties. Dry air and draughts are not tolerated and can cause excessive leaf drop. Too much water or insufficient warmth can cause plants literally to fade away.

Mature plants can grow to about 30cm (1ft) in height with leaves about 10cm (4in) wide.

Position A position of good light, but not direct sunlight is best.
Temperature All plants need a minimum temperature of about 13°C (55°F).
Watering Water every 10 days during the summer months and about every 14-18 days in winter.
Feeding Feed half the recommended dose every three weeks during the summer.
Pests and disease The red spider mite can infest the plant.

Philodendron scandens.

PHILODENDRON SCANDENS*
(Sweetheart plant)
Philodendron scandens was introduced into Britain in 1793 from the West Indies and Panama. In its native habitat it climbs up mossy tree trunks.

The plant can either be a trailer or climber; when trained to grow up a moss covered support the leaves can grow to a much larger size. The foliage is very handsome with exquisite heart-shaped leaves.

To encourage further stems, pinch out growing tips; remove any long, straggly growth in the spring.

Humidity and an even warm temperature best suits the plant. Spray regularly to increase humidity. They are quite hardy and there is much less likelihood of them losing their leaves or of them turning yellow than with other tropical houseplants.

Position Shady positions are preferred. This plant is happiest in a corner.

Temperature A minimum temperature of 15°C (60°F) is required.

Watering Water twice a week in summer but only once a week in winter.

Feeding Feed every two weeks during the summer months and not at all during the winter.

Pests and disease Greenfly, mealy bugs and red spider mites can sometimes attack.

PILEA CADIEREI***
(Aluminium plant)

This is the most popular of the pileas. It was first discovered in the forests of Vietnam and brought into France in 1938. It gets its common name from the metallic sheen on the white areas of the leaves – it looks as though it has been painted with liquid aluminium. This small, ornamental foliage plant is not too difficult to grow well.

A humid atmosphere is preferred; daily spraying with soft water will help. Pileas like a warm atmosphere but not overwatering, especially in the growing season.

If the plants are kept for too long they begin to look unattractive and rapidly deteriorate, so make new plants from cuttings every three or four years. Another form of *Pilea cadierei* is *P.c. nana*, a compact, bushy plant which only grows to about 30cm (1ft) in height. It has pretty silver and green spear-shaped leaves.

Position Prefers a position of good light but not direct sunlight.

Temperature Keep the plant at a minimum temperature of about 10°C (50°F).

Watering Water two to three times a week in summer.

Feeding Feed every two weeks during the summer months.

Pests and disease Can suffer from mould rot and greenfly.

Pilea cadierei

RHOICISSUS RHOMBOIDEA*
(Grape ivy, Natal ivy)

This ivy is an attractive climbing plant and thrives particularly well in shady corners. As one of its common names suggests it comes from Natal in South Africa. The leaves are shiny, dark green and diamond shaped. When the leaves and shoots first appear they are covered in brown hairs.

You can train rhoicissus to grow up a single support or it can be encouraged to produce several new shoots which turn it into a much more bushy plant. The plant can grow to at least 1.5m (5ft) and could even go higher. It does not like direct sun or too much light which can make the leaves turn a sickly yellow colour and even drop. It grows quickly and will need repotting every spring – sometimes, when young, even in the summer as well. Eventually it will be quite happy in a pot 23cm (9in) in diameter.

Position A slightly shaded position is preferred.

Temperature 10°C (50°F) is about the minimum temperature for *rhoicissus*.

Watering Water twice a week during the summer months.

Pests and disease Can be prone to greenfly and red spider mites.

SANSEVIERIA TRIFASCIATA*
(Mother-in-law's tongue)

The distinctive, upright leaves of this plant are green, edged with yellow. They resemble swords and grow to be about 30-45cm (1-1½ft) tall and about 5cm (2in) wide, clustering together and becoming quite dense in plants which are well grown. The leaves are also fleshy and if you overwater them they can start to rot at the base. Otherwise, they cope extremely well – even in conditions of bad treatment and neglect.

As sansevierias originate from Africa and Asia they like plenty of light and sun plus steady warmth.

In West Africa, this particular species is still used for hemp, which is made from the fibres in the leaves.

Sansevieras will flower in late spring if in the right conditions. The flowers are small and greenish-white, in the form of a spike, and have a lovely fragrance.

Position A light, sunny position is best, well away from draughts.

Temperature 10°C (50°F) is the minimum temperature preferred.

Watering Ensure that you do not overwater; water every 7-10 days during the summer months and every two weeks during the winter.

Feeding Feed every three weeks throughout the summer.

Pests and disease Mealy bugs and grey mould are a problem.

SAXIFRAGA STOLONIFERA*
(Mother of thousands)
The rest of the saxifrage family mainly consists of small rock plants, with closely packed leaves and which flower in the spring. *Saxifraga stolonifera*, which is cultivated in a pot, is very different. It has quite large dark green and white hairy leaves which are kidney-shaped. In early summer, small white flowers with gold centres appear on 15cm (6in) stems and numerous plantlets are produced at the ends of long runners – hence the common name Mother of thousands. These runners can either be cut off to make new plants or they can trail down prettily from a hanging basket.

A variety called 'Tricolour' has leaves with an uneven cream edge; the stems and young leaves are a pink colour. A lovely plant, it grows slowly and needs warmth and light, but is well worth the effort.

Position Likes a site with good light.

Temperature Minimum temperature should be about 10°C (50°F). The plant will tolerate extremely low temperatures for short periods of time.

Watering Keep moist throughout the year; if kept slightly drier in spring and summer flowering will be encouraged.

Feeding Survives well without feeding.

Pests and disease Not particularly troubled by pests but occasionally is disturbed by greenfly and white fly.

SCHEFFLERA ACTINOPHYLLA*
(Umbrella tree)
These are elegant plants with large, palmate, shiny leaves. The genus was named after the Danish botanist J.C. Scheffler and comes from Indonesia, northern Australia and New Zealand.

The plant can grow to more than 1.8m (6ft) tall in a pot. Steady temperatures are very important; they must not fall below 10°C (50°F) in winter and not rise above 16°C (60°F). Otherwise the plant will become weak and straggly and may be attacked by scale insects.

Draughts and direct sunlight should be avoided as they cause leaf drop; this will also occur if the temperature falls too low in the winter. In summer more humidity is preferred and the leaves will benefit from an occasional sponging.

Position Good light, but not direct sunlight, is best.

Temperature The minimum temperature that is suitable is 10°C (50°F).

Watering Water two or three times a week in summer and once a week in winter.

Feeding Feed half the recommended dose every two weeks in summer.

Pests and disease Red spider mites, scale insects and mealy bugs can attack.

SCINDAPSUS AUREUS**
(Devil's ivy)
The devil's ivy was first introduced from the Solomon Islands. It is a climbing plant which has attractive and unusual heart-shaped foliage.

There are two brightly-coloured varieties called 'Marble Queen' and 'Golden Queen'. Marble Queen is variegated so extensively with white that only flecks of green can be seen. Golden Queen is similar except that it has yellow variegation rather than white. Both species grow slowly and need plenty of warmth and light. All plants have tiny aerial roots and will benefit from a sphagnum moss or bark-covered support into which the roots can penetrate.

Position Likes good light but not direct sunlight.

Temperature Minimum temperature is 10°C (50°F) for the devil's ivy.

Watering Water every four to five days in summer and once a week in winter.

Feeding Feed half the recommended dose every two weeks in summer.

Pests and disease Red spider mites can infest the plant.

Scindapsus aureus

SYNGONIUM (NEPHTHYTIS) PODOPHYLLUM**
(Goosefoot plant)

The Goosefoot plant is an evergreen climber which originates from Central America. It is a rather slow climber and tends to form a stalked cluster of leaves from which a central stem gradually emerges.

The most popular variety is 'Emerald Gem' which has leaves with a silvery-green colouring. As they mature the leaves divide into three to form the goosefoot shape, with the veins outlined in white.

Position They prefer bright, direct light but not hot sun.

Temperature The minimum temperature should be about 15°C (60°F) for this plant.

Watering Two to three times a week in summer but only once a week in winter.

Feeding Feed half the recommended dose every three weeks during the summer months.

Pests and disease Greenfly and red spider mites can be a problem.

TRADESCANTIA*
(Wandering Jew)

Tradescantias are easy-to-grow trailing plants which come from South America. They were named after John Tradescant, a gardener to Charles I, and introduced into Europe in the seventeenth century. They can be propagated from almost any piece of stem and look their best when several plants are

Tradescantia

grouped together in a hanging basket.
Position Needs a position of good light.
Temperature A minimum temperature of 10°C (50°F) is required.
Watering Water twice a week in summer.
Feeding Feed every two weeks during the summer months.
Pests and disease Greenfly is the pest that can cause trouble.

ZEBRINA PENDULA*

This plant is very closely related to the tradescantia and is often called by the same common name. It, too, is easy to grow and has brightly-coloured foliage which is the same shape as that of the tradescantia but tends to be slightly larger and is striped silvery green, dark green and purple.
Position A position of good light is ideal.
Temperature The minimum temperature recommended is about 10°C (50°F).
Watering Water twice a week in summer, less in winter.
Feeding Feed every two weeks during the summer months.
Pests and disease Again, greenfly can be a problem.

Zebrina pendula

FERNS

These attractive plants were first grown in the home in Wardian cases in the Victorian era. They lost popularity at the beginning of this century but now, with centrally heated homes – which particularly suit them – they are making a comeback. Some species can be bought in florist shops, others have to be searched out. Either way you will be more than rewarded with your final choice.

ADIANTUM**
(Maidenhair fern)
This is a quite untypical fern: it has rounded, green leaves and thin, strong stems. But the raised brown spots under the leaves give it away – they are the fern spores. All the plants need a lot of humidity; it is essential for the delicate fronds.

Adiantum capillus-veneris is the British species which grows well and easily as a houseplant. *A. raddianum* is a very similar plant but larger and taller, reaching about 50cm (20in) in height.
Position They like good light but not direct sunlight.
Temperature Temperature 7°C (45°F) is the recommended temperature for these plants.
Watering Water well and spray daily.
Feeding Feed half the normal dose every two weeks in the summer.
Pests and disease Resistant to most pests and disease.

ASPARAGUS PLUMOSUS*
(Asparagus fern)
This is the fern that is commonly used in corsages and wedding bouquets. The small form, *Asparagus p. nanus* is the best plant to grow in the home because it does not grow too tall. *A. densiflorus* is commonly grown, it has trailing stems and delicate, needle-like leaves. All the varieties originate from South Africa but do not need a good heat to survive as one would expect.
Position Equally happy in shade or light, but the plant will not tolerate direct sunlight.
Temperature The minimum temperature required is 7°C (45°F).
Watering Water well two to three times a week in summer and once a week in winter.
Feeding Feed half the normal dose every two weeks in summer.
Pests and disease Scale insects and red spider mites can infest the plant.

DAVALLIA*
(Squirrel's foot fern, Hare's foot fern)

Davillia bullata has furry rhizomes which give the plant its common name of Squirrel's foot fern. These spread quickly and produce many triangular, dark green fronds. The plant tolerates a dry atmosphere very well and is happy in a centrally heated home.

D. canariensis is a small species with thick brown rhizomes. The fronds are fine, leathery and mid-green in colour. *D. fijiensis* grows much more freely. The fronds are larger but more delicate and are a lighter green colour.

Position Tolerates a little sunlight and thrives in a light position.

Temperature A minimum temperature of 5°C (41°F) is needed.

Watering Should be kept moist throughout the year, but particularly during the summer.

Feeding Follow care instructions carefully.

Adiantum

NEPHROLEPSIS EXALTATA*
(Ladder fern)
A hanging basket really shows off to advantage this attractive and deservedly popular fern. It is found in the tropical areas of the world and therefore needs warmth throughout the year. The fronds are cut and well divided and on an average plant can grow up to 1.8m (6ft) long. *Nephrolepsis cordifolia,* is a smaller species and the light green fronds only attain a length of about 60cm (2ft).

Like most ferns, both of these species need plenty of humidity and watering with soft water.

Position Good light or a little shade is preferred.

Temperature A minimum temperature of about 10°C (50°F) is needed.

Watering Keep moist throughout the year but water more frequently in summer.

Feeding Feed once a week during the summer months.

PELLAEA ROTUNDIFOLIA**
(Button fern)
This is a very pretty fern which originates from New Zealand. True to its name, it has rounded leaves which alternate in pairs along the fronds' stems. The fronds grow to about 30cm (12in) long and trail toward the ground so they can be very effective in a plant display.

The button-shaped leaves are rather waxy and dark green on the top with a lighter green underneath. When the plant is mature the shape of the leaves is more oblong.

The Button fern is quite tolerant of its surroundings and gets its own humidity from its surrounding potting mixture.

P. viridis is another species of this fern. It is upright and bushy. The fronds grow up to 75cm (30in) long. This plant is ideal for offices as it thrives under fluorescent lighting.

Position Thrives well in shade and indirect natural light; does not like draughts.

Ferns can be grown in Wardian cases

Fern balls are a lovely way of showing off your plants

Temperature A minimum temperature of about 7°C (45°F) is required for this plant.
Watering Water freely in summer but keep the compost just moist in winter.
Feeding Feed once a week during the summer months, not at all during the winter.

PTERIS**
(Silver lace fern, Trembling fern)
Several different species of this plant are cultivated. *Pteris ensitormis* is an attractive plant with short fronds which tend to be bushy. They are variegated with white stripes on the main vein and down the pinna, and can reach 50cm (20in) in length.

    P. tremula (trembling fern) is a fast growing fern which, given the right conditions, can reach over 1m (3ft) in height. The foilage is yellowy green, the feathery blades are triangular and the pinnae are deeply serrated.
Position A shaded or position of natural light is preferred away from direct sunlight.
Temperature A minimum temperature of about 10°C (50°F) is recommended.
Watering Water as often as once a day in summer but only twice a week in winter.
Feeding Feed half the normal dose every two weeks in the summer months.
Pests and disease Scale insects and grey mould can be a problem.

PALMS

There is no doubt that palms exude an aura of elegance and style in whatever setting they are placed. They can look extremely majestic dominating a corner of a living room, for example. A palm in an ornamental pot on a high stand can also be very attractive. Palms tend to be mature plants which have been carefully nurtured before they can be seen at their best. They are very popular despite being expensive – the high cost is because of the time and high heating costs involved in rearing them properly.

CHAMAEDORA ELEGANS*
(Parlour palm)
The parlour palm is a delightful miniature palm when young and is particularly suitable for smaller rooms, bottle gardens or even dish gardens as it seems quite content to live in these rather cramped conditions.

When the mature plant grows to a height of about 1.2m (4ft) tall. The plant has a languid air as its fine, narrow leaves are suspended on dropping fronds and stems. The leaves are about 13cm (5in) in length and feathery in appearance. The fronds tend to be about 30cm (12in) long.

Occasionally – in a hot, humid summer – a mature parlour palm might produce flowers which look like yellow plumes; small, shiny fruits follow.

Position The parlour palm likes strong, natural light but not direct sun.

Temperature A minimum temperature of 13°C (55°F) is required.

Watering Water two to three times a week during the summer months and once a week in the winter.

Feeding Feed every two weeks during the summer months with half the normal dose.

Pests and disease Red spider mites can infest the plant.

CHRYSALIDOCARPUS LUTESCENS*
(Areca palm, Butterfly palm)
A native of Mauritius and the Tropics, this adaptable palm is a very graceful plant. It has feathery foilage, the leaves of which form a fan shape.

When the plant is fully mature it grows to a height of about 6m (20ft) but, for obvious reasons, it tends to be a houseplant when it is younger and around 1.2-2.5m (4-8ft) tall. The stems and leaves have an unusual yellow tinge and on a normal sized plant the fronds can grow to quite a length, often about 90cm

(3ft). The stems of older plants have ring marks where leaves have grown previously.

New leaves are extremely attractive as they are joined together at their tips. Watching them opening can be fascinating. The plant should be repotted during Spring.

Position Bright, natural sunlight but away from draughts is ideal.

Temperature A minimum temperature of about 18°C (65°F) is needed.

Watering The soil should be kept moist throughout the year but water less in winter. The roots must never be allowed to stand in excess water in the pot holder.

Feeding Feed once a week during the summer months from April to late September.

Chamaedora elegans

CYCAS REVOLUTA**
(Sago palm)
This is one of the oldest and most majestic of the palm family.
The mature plant reaches a height of at least 1.8m (6ft) and has
a large trunk which makes it look very formidable. Leaves are
stiff and dark green in colour, with very thin individual
segments which bend over slightly at their tips.

This is not the plant for you if you want one that grows
rapidly in the year – only a few leaves appear annually and the
rate of growth is extremely slow.

The sago palm must never dry out as it needs plenty of
moisture and likes a loam-based soil mixture.

Position Good light is important but strong sunlight should be
avoided.

Temperature The minimum temperature for this plant is
about 15°C (60°F).

Watering Keep moist throughout the year.

Feeding Follow care instructions and feed during the summer
months.

Pests and disease Can occasionally be bothered by red spider
mites and scale insects.

HOWEIA**
(Kentia)
The natural habitat of howeias is the Lord Howe Island in the
Pacific. Kentia is the capital town of the island and was used,
until recently, as the botanic name for the palms. One species
still retains the name Kentia for its common name.

These are still very popular palms despite the fact there are
only a few being cultivated and these are obviously very
expensive.

Howeias have feathery, graceful leaves, in time growing
into big plants several metres tall, which can be quite
imposing.

Howeia forsteriana grows very straight and is therefore
better as a houseplant than *H. belmoreana*. Although the plant
is generally very tolerant the dark green leaves can be damaged
by chemical mixtures used to clean other plants without any
adverse effect. It can be seen at its best when two or three
plants are grown together. Single plants can grow to a height
of 4.5m (15ft) but when several are grouped together the
growth is less.

Position Howeias like some light but survive very well in
shaded positions.

Temperature The minimum temperature recommended is
about 10°-13°C (50-55°F).

Watering Keep moist throughout the year, particularly during
the summer.

Feeding Follow care instructions and feed regularly during the
summer months.

PHOENIX*

The two varieties of this palm which are sold as houseplants are *Phoenix canariensis* and *P. roebelenii.* The latter comes from South-east Asia and is the more graceful plant; it can really add elegance to a room. *P. canariensis* (Canary date palm), as its name suggests, originates from the Canary Islands. In the tropics both plants are grown as decorative trees but they take many years to reach maturity if they are confined to opts. They can therefore be a very attractive feature of the home as they gradually change in size and shape over the years. The leaves of both are stiff and spiky.

Position Prefer good light and airy conditions.

Temperature The minimum temperature required is about 10°-13°C (50°-55°F).

Watering Water two to three times a week in summer but every two weeks in winter.

Feeding Feed every two weeks during the summer months.

Pests and disease Can be attacked by mealy bugs.

Phoenix palm

FLOWERING PLANTS

Flowers in the home always add wonderful colour and often fragrance but to have to buy cut flowers every week is an extravagance and perhaps time consuming. A flowering plant often lasts much longer – blooming for several weeks if not months; some will even flower all year round. There are also several varieties which burst into flower during the winter months, brightening up the home on those greyest of days.

ACHIMENES**
(Hot water plant)
Achimenes were introduced from Central and South America in the early 1800s. These pretty plants can either grow straight up or trail, and have tubular or trumpet-shaped flowers that bloom from mid-summer to early autumn. The plants come in many different colours, the main ones being purple, blue, violet and rose-pink. The common name came about when people thought the plant had to be watered with hot water; water at room temperature, however, is quite sufficient.

Easy varieties to grow are 'Purple King', the deep crimson 'Queen of Sheba' and 'Tourmaline', which is pink with yellow and purple markings.
Position A sunny window is ideal but shade from hot sun.
Temperature The minimum temperature recommended is 13°C (55°F).
Watering Keep moist throughout the growing season.
Feeding Feed recommended dose during the growing season.
Pests and disease Not usually troubled.

ALLAMANDA NERIIFOLIA**
This is a very shrubby flowering plant which needs a lot of space to grow in plus plenty of water and fertilizer. The leaves are mid-green in colour and lance shaped. In the spring, the plant bears small, bright yellow flowers which are rather dwarfed by the size of the plant. It can grow to a height of about 1.2m (4ft) and by this time will probably need a container 25cm (10in) wide. It is definitely not a plant for the small room as it would tend to completely dominate it.
Position The plant prefers a place where it is quite shady, away from draughts.
Temperature The minimum temperature required is 13°C (55°F).
Watering Water freely in spring and summer but keep fairly dry during the winter months.
Feeding Feed as detailed in the care instructions.
Pests and disease Not usually troubled.

Anthurium scherzerianum

ANTHURIUM SCHERZERIANUM***
(Flamingo plant)

Brilliant red, pink or sometimes white flowers adorn this unusual, attractive species. The flowers have a single, large petal with a coiled or straight spadix and grow on a stem 30-60cm (1-2ft) tall above shiny, green spear or heart-shaped leaves. They belong to the same family as the wild cuckoo pint or lords and ladies which are found in hedgerows.

Anthuriums come from the tropical rain forests of South America and therefore need plenty of humidity, adequate watering and warmth of soil and air. The main flowering season is the spring but they can go on blooming throughout the year.

Position Needs a position of good light but not direct sun.
Temperature The room temperature for this plant should not fall below 13°C (55°F).
Watering Water twice a week during the summer months and once a week during the winter.
Feeding Feed every two weeks during the summer months.
Pests and disease Mealy bugs, red spider mites and fungus can attack the plant.

APHELANDRA SQUARROSA**
(Zebra plant, Saffron spike)

A bright yellow flower spike and delicately striped foliage give this plant its common names. In Brazil, where it comes from, the zebra plant is a bushy evergreen shrub and grows to 1-2m (3-6ft) tall. The plants can normally be bought in early winter. Always make sure you get one with bracts that are only just beginning to separate as it will then flower for a long time. Plenty of humidity is needed; spraying the foliage every two or three days will help. Keep the plant out of draughts or it will start to lose its leaves.

The plant should be kept in a loam based soil because of its mass of roots.

The variety 'Louisae' can reach a height of about 60cm (2ft) while 'Dania' is a smaller and more compact, with silvery foliage.

Position Likes some light but keep out of the midday sun.

Temperature The minimum temperature for this plant is 10°C (50°F).

Watering Water two to three times a week in the summer months and once a week in winter. The soil must be kept permanently moist.

Feeding Feed every two weeks when the flower spike appears, and once a week when the plant is not in flower.

Pests and disease Red spider mites, greenfly and scale insects can attack.

Azalea indica

AZALEA INDICA*

(Azalea)

Azaleas are really lovely flowering plants. They have pink or red double flowers which are frilled and look like crumpled tissue paper. The plants originate in Japan – many of the first azaleas came from the Emperor's garden in Tokyo. The indoor azaleas suitable for houseplants are small evergreens which are quite hardy and do not need high temperatures but require adequate watering to stop them drying out.

The plants can be put out in the garden for the summer months and brought in again in the autumn in good time for the flowering period – from December. When buying, always choose a plant with plenty of ripening buds to ensure a long flowering period.

Position Likes a position of good light.

Temperature The plant's temperature must not fall below 10°-15°C (50°-60°F).

Watering Plunge in a bucket of tepid water twice weekly when in flower.

Feeding Feed every two weeks in summer.

Pests and disease Can be troubled by red spider mites.

BEGONIA**

Begonias get their name from Michel Begon, a French administrator and keen amateur botanist who was sent to the French Antilles in 1681 and brought back begonia samples to Europe. Many plants grow from tubers, others are fibrous rooted and have shoots and stems all the year round. Some have big double flowers while others have only small ones but might flower throughout the year, so a beautiful display of flowering pot plants all year round can be achieved by having several different species and hybrids.

Begonia sutherlandii is a small-flowered begonia, its massed orange flowers surrounding the plant. Even more flowers emerge from the rounded mound of leaves. It is quite a tolerant plant but needs a lot of watering when flowering. German rieger begonias are a fairly modern strain whose flowers are a cross between the large hybrids and the small flowering species. They flower from spring until winter and are found in glorious reds, oranges and pinks.

Position A position of good light is needed. This plant dislikes a stuffy atmosphere.

Temperature A minimum temperature of 13°C (55°F) is required for the plants.

Watering Water well when the plants are flowering but keep fairly dry at other times.

Feeding Feed once a week when flowering with a dilute solution of plant food.

Pests and disease Mildew can be a problem.

BELOPERONE GUTTATA*
(Shrimp plant)

The shrimp plant with its pinky orange 'flowers' shaped like shrimps will bloom all the year round if you let it. It is better to stop feeding it in the late autumn so that it is forced to rest for a few weeks; otherwise it will become very weak in the winter. The real flowers are small and white, spotted with purple, and emerge from between the orange bracts. Another variety called 'Yellow Queen' has yellow bracts.

This is a very ornamental plant and tolerant of all conditions, be it sun, shade, good light or watering. Give less water when you stop feeding it at the end of the autumn. At the end of the winter you can cut it back to half its size, pot in new compost and start it off again.

Position Likes full sunlight in summer but only indirect light in winter.

Temperature The minimum temperature recommended for this plant is 7°C (45°F).

Watering Water once or twice a week in summer but only every two weeks in winter.

Feeding Feed every two weeks during the summer months and not at all during the winter.

Pests and disease Can be bothered by red spider mites and greenfly.

CALCEOLARIA**
(Slipper flower)

Calceolarias are very unusual looking plants that come from Peru. They have pouched flowers that look rather like slippers or purses. The flowers are very exotic, about 5cm (2in) across and come in beautiful shades of red, pink, maroon, orange or yellow, dotted with contrasting spots. The leaves are soft and hairy to the touch. The plant blooms from May to July and flourishes most of all in conditions that are cool and airy; it will suffer in hot temperatures. When small plants are first bought they will benefit greatly if they are repotted straight away into a loam-based mixture. This cuts down the need to feed the plant and helps it to retain its rich green colouring. When the plants have finished flowering they should be thrown away.

Most calceolarias are hybrids and do not produce seeds.

Position A bright location with indirect sunlight is best. Avoid draughts.

Temperature Do not let this fall below a minimum of about 10°-15°C (50°-60°F).

Watering Keep the soil wet at all times but take care not to wet the leaves.

Feeding No feeding is necessary if the plant has been potted in a loam-based mixture.

Pest and disease Keep a look out for greenfly.

CALENDULA OFFINALIS*
(Pot marigold)

The exuberant colour of potted marigolds always brightens up the dullest corners. These very hardy plants are available in lemon yellow and gold as well as pure orange and they are not expensive. The leaves are oval shaped and the flowers are round and made up of many tiny petals. They do not like the heat, however, and should be found a suitable cool place where they can thrive.

The plants are in flower most of the year. If flowering is not too late in the year they can be de-headed and planted out in the garden where they might well produce another glorious patch of flowers.

Plenty of sun ensures short sturdy plants, as does pinching out the top shoot.

Position A position of good light is ideal. A window box is very suitable.

Temperature This plant is very tolerant and will survive in most temperatures.

Watering Keep the soil moist at all times, particularly during the summer.

Feeding Follow care instructions carefully.

Pests and disease Can be troubled by greenfly.

Calceolaria

CAMELLIA JAPONICA**

For a long time camellias were considered too difficult to care for when, in fact, they are quite hardy. They are evergreen shrubs with handsome, glossy dark green leaves and beautiful wax-like flowers and will grow for a long time in quite small pots. They thrive very well on north facing windows provided they are protected from draughts.

The best time to buy camellias is just after Christmas; a plant with plenty of buds will bloom for about two months. If you want the plant to produce large flowers, pinch off all the buds except one in each group. When it has finished flowering keep in a cool place and then plant it out in the garden when there is no likelihood of frost.

Position Likes a window position with good light but no draughts.

Temperature The minimum temperature recommended for this plant is about 10°-15°C (50°-60°F).

Watering Water well when the plant is flowering.

Feeding Feed every two weeks during the summer months.

CAMPANULA ISOPHYLLA*

(Italian Bellflower)

This lovely flowering plant comes from Italy. It has purple or white bell-shaped flowers, 2.5cm (1in) wide, which open out into star formations, and bloom from mid summer to late autumn. This is an easy-to-grow plant and can look very attractive in a hanging basket as it trails down.

The plant is a biennial so when it has finished growing, cut off the trailing stems and keep in a cool place for the winter months watering it only occasionally.

Position Needs a position of good light.

Camellia japonica

Chrysanthemum

Temperature A minimum temperature of about 6°C (43°F) is best.
Watering Needs plenty of water when flowering so check daily, but only water every 7-10 days in the winter.
Feeding Feed every two weeks during the summer months.
Pests and disease Red spider mites and greenfly can be a problem.

CHRYSANTHEMUM*

Chrysanthemums originate in China and the name means 'yellow flower' – the first varieties were yellow in colour.

It is a bushy pot plant available in many beautiful colours: yellow, crimson, deep pink and white. It is now bred to be available throughout the year. Choose a plant which has only three or four flowers that are out but which has a mass of green buds. When in flower the plant needs plenty of water and should be kept in a cool place with plenty of light. When flowering is finished cut the plant back but continue watering. Side shoots will then be produced and the ones closest to the soil can be used as cuttings for new plants; it can also be planted out in the garden.
Position Likes a lot of light but keep away from hot sun.
Temperature Temperatures should not fall below 4°-13°C (40°-55°F).
Watering Water every day
Feeding No feeding is necessary.
Pests and diseases Chrysanthemum virus can bother the plant.

CINERARIA*

Usually grown as a biennial, this attractive half-hardy perennial – with its daisy-like flowers in a glorious choice of colours – is the result of years of breeding and selection. Its parentage involves *Senecio cruentus*, a native to the Canary Islands.

Plants can be bought between early winter and spring; buy them when the buds are just beginning to show a hint of colour and you will be able to enjoy their flowers for about six weeks. Choose from reds, pinks, blues and white or the 'Double Mixed' with its wonderful colour combinations. The densely-packed daisy heads top stems range from 38cm-76cm (15in-30in) in height. When in flower they prefer cool places and need a lot of water plus a humid atmosphere.

Position These plants need good light, but not direct sunlight which causes the leaves to silt.

Temperature A minimum temperature of 7°-10°C (40°-50°F) is required.

Watering The compost, which should be rich, loamy and well-drained, needs to be kept moist at all times. But take care not to overwater as this may cause the plant to collapse.

Feeding No feeding is necessary.

Pests and disease Particularly prone to greenfly.

CLEMATIS*

Clematis (pictured right) is a lovely, hardy, climbing plant which is very popular for the garden where it will happily climb up trellis work, walls or railings. As a houseplant it can be potted in a good sized pot and then grown up supporting trellis work or canes.

The variety *Clematis jackmanii*, which is deep purple, is the most well known colour but there is a wide choice to select from. The plants flower from May to September and do not require much pruning.

Position A sunny position is ideal.

Temperature A minimum temperature of about 15°C (59°F) is needed.

Watering Water regularly as it must not dry out.

Feeding Regular feeding during the summer months is needed.

Pests and disease Not often troubled by them.

CYCLAMEN**

The cyclamen is quite a modern plant, as the first species wasn't introduced from North Africa, Cyprus, Turkey, Southern France and the Lebanon until the end of the last century. The name comes from the Greek *kyklos* meaning circular; the round seedheads of some species are pulled down onto the soil by the coiling of the stems in the same way as a spring..

The plants can flower in autumn, winter or early spring. All the varieties have small flowers which are about 1.3cm (½in) long. They come in many different colours: pink, rose, red, purple and white and some have lovely scents. The leaves are rounded and either green, silvery green or a white mottled colour. Cyclamen need an average temperature, a humid atmosphere and plenty of water to thrive. A smoky atmosphere or draughts will cause the leaves to discolour and wilt. Overwatering will cause the leaves to turn yellow and the corm may rot or a grey mould will attack.

Position A position of good light but away from bright sun is needed.

Temperature About 18°C (65°F) is the recommended temperature for this plant.

Watering Water with tepid water every day.

Feeding Feed every two weeks during the growing season.

Pests and disease Can be attacked by greenfly and botrytis.

Clematis

CYTISUS***
(Broom)

The hybrid *Cytisus racemosus* is a very attractive variety which is also compact enough to be grown as a houseplant. It is an evergreen with bright, golden-yellow flowers which bloom from winter to early summer.

It will grow to over 1.5m (5ft) tall in a large pot but it can be kept smaller by pinching back the shoots after the plant has flowered. The greyish-green foliage is very pleasing and the small flowers give off a lovely sweet fragrance. Buy it when the buds are just beginning to show a hint of colour.

The hybrid *C.x beanii* is a small and trailing variety not much more than 30cm (12in) high and 90cm (36in) across. It flowers in spring with golden-yellow blossom. *C. nigricans* is much later flowering (in July to September) and should be pruned hard back, but not into very old wood, in late spring. Seeds germinate freely but are not necessarily true to type.

Position Needs a position of good light but shield from direct sun in the summer.

Temperature A minimum temperature of about 7°C (45°F) is required.

Watering Water more freely during the summer months and spray regularly.

Feeding Feed moderately during the growing season. If you overfeed them, they will become very leafy at the expense of the flowers.

Cyclamen

ERICA***
(Heath, heather)

There are actually more than five hundred species of heather but only about 16 come from Europe – the rest originate in South Africa and are therefore not that hardy in the British climate.

The species that are grown as houseplants are normally available at Christmas. *Erica gracilis*, from South Africa, grows to about 45cm (1½ft) tall and is available with pink or white heather-shaped flowers. It is not certain where *E. hiemalis* originates from but it is commonly known as the Cape heath. Its tubular flowers are pink with white tips. The plants normally bloom from October to January. An airy, cool room with plenty of light is ideal. They should not be allowed to dry out and, ideally, should be watered with soft water or rain water. Misting with a fine spray every day is also essential to keep the atmosphere humid.

Position Plenty of light is best but keep out of draughts.

Temperature A minimum temperature of about 5°C (41°F) is required.

Watering Do not let the plant dry out but keep moist at all times; water daily when flowering.

Feeding Follow care instructions carefully.

Pests and disease Virtually untroubled by pests and disease.

EUPHORBIA PULCHERRIMA**
(Poinsettia)

The poinsettia is a native of Mexico and was first brought into Europe in 1834. Cultivated as a houseplant since about 1950, this attractive evergreen is normally available at Christmas. It can grow to about 3m (10ft) in height. As a member of the spurge family the plant's stems contain a milky fluid which trickles out when they are cut. In some species this can be poisonous but it is harmless in the poinsettia.

Poinsettias are more hardy than they used to be, thanks to further breeding and selection. The red 'flowers' are not petals but bracts; the real flowers are tiny and yellow in the centre of the bract. The leaves are lobed, quite large and light green. The most usual flower colour is red, but pink or white plants can be bought. A steady, warm temperature, humidity, no draughts and good light are necessary for poinsettias. They also need to be carefully watered to keep the compost moist but not wet.

Position Needs a position of good light but with no draughts.

Temperature Do not let the plant's temperature fall below 13°C (55°F).

Watering Water twice a week when in flower, then leave almost dry for a month before resuming watering, once a week.

Feeding Feed every two weeks when growing.

Pests and disease Can be attacked by greenfly and silver leaf virus.

EXACUM AFFINE*
(Arabian violet, Persian violet)
Exacum affine is a member of the Gentian family. It reaches a height of about 23cm (9in) and is a neat plant covered in shiny, green, oval-shaped leaves and purple, yellow-centred fragrant flowers which bloom from early summer until mid to late autumn.

The plant comes from Socotra, an island in the Gulf of Aden and although it is grown as a perennial there, in houseplant form it is an annual which should be discarded in late autumn when it has finished flowering. A warm atmosphere with plenty of light and some humidity is preferred by the plant and will keep it flowering. Too much light, particularly hot sun, can be detrimental – causing the edges of the leaves to go brown.

Position Good light is essential but avoid direct sun.
Temperature The minimum required temperature is 16°-18°C (60°-65°F).
Watering Make sure the compost is moist at all times.
Feeding Feed once a week during the summer months and flowering period.
Pests and diseases Not particularly affected by pests and disease.

FUCHSIA**
(Lady's eardrops)
Lovely, unusual bell-shaped flowers adorn this easy-to-cultivate plant. Fuchsias originate from Central and South America and New Zealand and were named after the sixteenth century botanist, Leonhart Fuchs. They were particularly popular in Victorian times when they were grown in conservatories. They are still popular today and there are specialist fuchsia societies with many members.

Many varieties of fuchsia are grown; the typical plant flower has a tubular centre of purple petals, surrounded by an outer cap of rosy pink petals, with long stamens drooping from the centre. In some forms the tube is doubled and colours can vary from purple or red to white. The flowering period is from mid-April to August. A cool position with a little shade and a good deal of humidity most suits fuchsias.

They look particularly attractive in hanging baskets where they can trail down and the beauty of the flowers can really be appreciated.

Position Put in a position of good light but not direct sunlight.
Temperature The minimum temperature recommended is about 7°C (45°F).
Watering Water three to four times a week in summer; can dry out in winter.
Feeding Feed weekly when blooming.
Pests and disease Greenfly can infest the plant.

GLOXINIA**
(Sinningia speciousa)

Gloxinias are glorious looking plants both for the plush foliage and the flowers which are velvety and trumpet shaped. They come in many different colours, including pink, rose, purple, red, blue and white. Some varieties, called tigrina gloxinias, have spotted or veined, coloured flowers on a white background and they have frilly edges.

The plants come from the forests of Brazil and Argentina and need conditions of good light, steady warmth and plenty of humidity. Watering should always be done with soft, tepid water as it is very important not to chill the compost which would damage the plant. Always water at the edge of the pot.

Position Good light is essential but keep out of the midday sun.

Temperature The temperature should not fall below 16°C (60°F) for this plant.

Watering Water from the bottom of the plant two to three times a week in summer but allow to dry out in the winter.

Feeding Feed once a week during the summer with potash-high fertilizer.

Pests and disease Greenfly and spotted wilt can both be problems.

Fuchsia

HYDRANGEA MACROPHYLLA*
(Hydrangea)

Lovely, bright clusters of flowers appear on this plant. They can be various colours but what is intriguing is the way the flowers change colour, depending on the amount of acid present in the soil.

Hydrangeas originate in Japan and North America and are usually bought as houseplants when they are about 45-60cm (18-24in) tall. They are hardy plants with shiny, oval leaves and clusters of individual flowers. The colour of the flowers can be deep blue, vivid purple, red, soft pink, pale blue and even white. The plants bloom in spring and the flowers last for about six weeks. The flower clusters are made up of male and female florets, some of them fertile. The infertile florets tend to be the most showy. When watering use rainwater as the plants can react adversely to tap water.

After flowering you can put the plants in your garden or maybe a large tub outside. They will then increase in size and continue to flower.

Position Like a position of good light.

Temperature The minimum temperature should be about 7°C (45°F).

Watering Immerse in a bucket of tepid water three times a week during the summer but water only every 10 days in winter.

Feeding Feed every week when the plant is flowering.

Pests and disease Red spider mites, greenfly and fungus can infest the plant.

Hydrangea

Impatiens

IMPATIENS*
(Busy lizzie)
How this plant ever got its common name is a mystery, but it
certainly does keep busy, as it flowers all the time.

Because of this it is a very popular plant, although its habit
of constantly dropping flowers puts some owners off.
However, this will not happen if the plant is kept
moist.

Impatiens walleriana comes from the tropical region of
Africa. The houseplants are hybrids and cultivars of the
tropical species and available in several colours – red, orange,
magenta, white or pink being the main ones. There are also
varieties which are variegated and white at the edges. The
medium-sized flowers are flat and the small leaves are oval
shaped.

The plants need a lot of water as the fleshy stems and rapid
growth indicate. Humidity is also important; the plants do not
like central heating. Too often you see Busy lizzies on hot
window sills surrounded by fallen flowers and possibly
infested by the red spider mite. Keep them only reasonably
warm and in quite a good light and they should do well.

Position Plenty of light is needed but keep out of direct
sunlight.

Temperature The minimum temperature for this plant should
be about 13°C (55°F).

Watering Water two to three times a week in summer but only
every 10 days in winter.

Feeding Feed once a week during the summer months and not
at all during the winter.

Pests and disease Greenfly, red spider mites and sooty mould
can be a problem.

PELARGONIUM*
(Geranium)

Geraniums have been very popular as houseplants for a long time. They seem to be very difficult to kill off and will still manage to produce flowers under the most difficult conditions. There are several different types of geranium; they include the regals with their big, single open trumpet-shaped flowers, the zonals, which have leaves with dark bands or zones and produce small flowers, and the miniature zonals which only grow to about 15cm (6in) tall.

The plants flower throughout the summer, with the exception of the regals which bloom in late spring to early summer for about a month. The plants come in a variety of colours, including pink, violet, red, mauve and maroon.

Position Place in a position of good, natural light. It is important to plant them in a standard compost with extra grit and a lot of drainage material at the base. Keep them away from draughts.

Temperature The minimum recommended temperature is about 10°C (50°F).

Watering Water two to three times a week in summer but only every two weeks in winter.

Feeding Feed every two weeks when the plant is growing.

Pests and disease White fly, fungus and leafy gall can attack the plant.

Pelargonium

PRIMULA ALCAULIS SYN PRIMULA VULGARIS*
(Primrose)

Primula vulgaris is basically the common primrose. They are hardy and survive in the coldest parts of the home. Some varieties are forced so that they appear before Christmas.

Position Likes a position of good light.
Temperature Needs a minimum temperature of 4°C (40°F).
Watering Water two to three times a week.
Feeding Feed once a week when flowering.
Pests and greenfly Can be attacked by greenfly.

ROSA CHINENSIS MINIMA*
(Pot rose, miniature rose)

These lovely miniature roses are the ideal solution if you adore roses but do not have a garden. They are quite hardy and grow to about 15-30cm (6-12in) high, flowering from early summer until autumn. The flowers are very small, but exact replicas of garden roses and some are fragrant.

Position Needs good light and some direct sunlight.
Temperature Needs a minimum temperature of 10°-18°C (50°-65°F).
Watering Keep the soil fairly moist.
Feeding Feed once a week during flowering period.
Pests and disease Keep a watch for greenfly and mildew.

Pelargoniums make excellent window-box displays.

SAINTPAULIA IONANTHA**

(African violet)

African violets come from the mountains of Tanzania in East Africa and they can be very frustrating as houseplants because they flower profusely for one person while simply producing glorious leaves for another – even when there are exactly the same conditions! They are available in pinks, purples, magentas, blues and whites; some have single blooms, others double or maybe frilly petals. The leaves can be either dark or light green. Flowering can be almost continuous from mid summer to late winter. Steady warmth is needed at all times.

Position Good light is necessary but keep out of direct sun.

Temperature Do not let the temperature fall below 13°C (55°F).

Watering Water from the bottom of the plant twice weekly throughout the year.

Feeding Feed every three to four weeks when growing.

Pests and disease Can be attacked by greenfly and mould.

STEPHANOTIS FLORIBUNDA***

(Madagascar jasmine)

A heavy, sweet fragrance distinguishes these pretty, white flowered plants, often used to make up wedding bouquets, corsages and button holes. The tubular flowers are produced in groups from spring and on and off through the summer months. They are evergreens which twine as they climb to as high as 4.5m (15ft). As a pot plant they can be trained to grow up canes. Careful pruning will keep them under control and encourage them to flower. Steady warmth and humidity are needed at all times.

Position Needs a lot of light.

Temperature A minimum temperature of 15°C (60°F) is recommended.

Saintpaulia ionantha

Watering Water two to three times a week in summer but only once a week in the winter.
Feeding Feed half the normal dose every two weeks in the summer.
Pests and disease Scale insects, red spider mites and mealy bugs can attack.

STREPTOCARPUS**

(Cape primrose)
Trumpet-shaped flowers cover these attractive pot plants, which are easy to cultivate but are not widely grown. The flowers are about 3.5cm (1½in) long and appear in ones or twos on slim stems which grow to about 10cm (4in). The leaves are long and strap-like and spread outwards, the flowers growing in the middle. Blue, violet, pink, red, white and lilac are the main colours.

 The plants are perennial and bloom from late spring until the autumn. Generally cool, well lit conditions are preferred with adequate humidity.
Position Likes plenty of light but keep out of the sun.
Temperature The minimum temperature needed is about 15°C (60°F).
Watering Water two to three times a week in summer but only once a week in winter.
Feeding Feed half the normal dose once a month.
Pests and disease Greenfly can infest the plant.

Streptocarpus

BULBS

The sight of a glorious display of spring bulb flowers in the home during late winter and early spring never fails to cheer everyone up.

They can be quite easy to grow inside, providing you choose healthy-looking ones and follow a few simple rules. They can be bought from florists or the gardening section of general stores and can even be bought in kit form together with suitable compost and container. The bulb actually contains, in embryonic form, the already formed leaves, stem and flower; all it needs are the right conditions to develop. Bulbs that will flower in mid winter have already been specially cultivated and kept under controlled conditions of humidity and temperature. You can force bulbs yourself by keeping the pots in the dark until roots form and then gradually bring them out into the light. Corms are swollen stem bases of plants; like bulbs, they have a base plate which produces the roots and top growth. The tubers are another form of storage organ – a modified stem with bubs; the nutrients are stored in the tuber for the next year's growth.

Most bulbs flower form late winter to late spring but some also flower in the summer. The most usual way of cultivating bulbs indoors is in bowls or similar containers.

To start your bulbs, half-fill a pot with damp bulb fibre and gently position the bulb or bulbs with the pointed tip upwards. The bulbs should then be covered if they are small – but leave the tip exposed on large ones – and moisten again. Leave in a

This attractive arrangement contains aconites, snowdrops and crocuses

dark and cool place – about 5°-7° (40°-45°F) – for about six to
twelve weeks, checking every two weeks that the fibre is still
moist. When the yellowish-green tips appear, move the
container into the light and a temperature of 10°C (50°F).
When the buds are showing, move to a warmer place, 16°C
(60°F) and leave the bulbs to produce their superb flowers.
Feeding is important; feed until the leaf tips turn yellow and
wither. Eel worm can devastate the plant; if yours has a
stunted bulb and misshapen flowers destroy it immediately.

CHIONODOXA*
(Glory of the snow)
The chionodoxa is a charming bulb plant which originates
from the eastern Mediterranean and the mountains of Crete
and western Turkey. It is worth planting a few bulbs in a
container in autumn and forcing them on so that they flower
in the middle of winter when summer seems so far away. The
flowers are bright blue and in the shape of stars. They grow in
clusters surrounded by narrow leaves. Other varieties have
pink or white flowers.

Pot the bulbs in late autumn in moist compost which is
about 2.5cm (1in) deep – about six will fit in an 8cm (3½in)
pot. Place them in a cold place, outdoors if possible, until the
beginning of winter so that they grow roots, and then start
giving them a higher temperature.

Water and feed them regularly after flowering until they
begin to die down. Leave them to dry out until autumn then
repot in new compost.

Chionodoxa

CLIVIA MINIATA*
(Kaffir lily)

The mountain valleys of Natal in South Africa are the Kaffir lily's place of origin. It is a spring plant that grows very easily and has bright orange, funnel-shaped flowers that grow in clusters. The plant reaches about 30-60cm (1-2ft) in height and has narrow, evergreen leaves. New leaves develop for the plant in pairs; a ten year-old plant may have as many as eight or nine flowerheads with perhaps a dozen flowers each.

Clivias do not form proper bulbs. Instead they build up layers of fleshy leaf bases which become rounded and bulb-like in time.

Varieties can now be bought which have red-orange or yellow flowers but all have yellow throats.

The temperature and watering are extremely important when you are cultivating this plant. In winter the temperature should not rise above 14°C (58°F) and, ideally, should be about 10°C (50°F). In summer more warmth is preferred, about 16°-21°C (60°-70°F). The Kaffir lily reacts strongly to over-watering; never allow water to collect in the bottom of the pot. Always give plenty of water in one session but then let the plant dry out before watering again. Between autumn and mid winter little water is needed.

Humidity is not particularly necessary but good light and some sun are best when the plant is flowering. The plant can be kept in the same pot for several years provided it is fed from spring until mid summer. Leaving the pot in the same position all the time encourages the best flowering. Spraying the plant from time to time removes dust and grime.

These plants will thrive in ordinary potting compost and young offsets should be potted in peaty compost.

A close look out should be kept for scale insects which can get in between the leaf bases and be very difficult to get rid of. Increase the plant by removing offsets when they have four to five leaves and pot singly into peaty compost in 7.5cm (3in) pots.

Bulbs should be potted close together, but not touching each other.

5°C / 40°F

The tips should be above the potting fibre which should be kept moist.

COLCHICUM*
(Naked boys)

Colchicum mainly flower in the autumn. They are tuber plants and have impressive, goblet-shaped flowers which resemble giant crocuses. The flowers appear before the leaves which grow on 30cm (1ft) stems and grow in the spring with the seedpods – this is how the common name originates.

The tubers should be planted during the late summer about 5cm (2in) deep in good potting soil and deep pots; water until moist. They can also actually flower successfully without soil or water but will deteriorate if not planted soon afterwards.

Colchicum autumnale has flowers with star-like petals which are either rosy-lilac or white. *C. speciosus* has more, much larger flowers which tend to be globe-shaped and rosy-purple in colour. Other cultivars from *C. speciosus* include 'Album' which has white flowers, 'Disraeli' with deep mauve flowers and distinctive markings, 'Waterlily' with rosy-mauve flowers and 'The Giant' with mauve-pink flowers with a white base. The plants normally grow to about 7.5-15cm (3-6in) in height.

C. luteum, which has yellow flowers about 2.5cm (1in) wide, flowers in the late winter.

CONVALLARIE MAJALIS*
(Lily-of-the-valley)

Lily-of-the-valley have lovely, small, sweet-smelling flowers suspended on arching stems and delicate, tall oval leaves. The plants can be forced to flower out of season. You can often buy them in bundles of 25 and they can be loosely planted together in peat or light soil.

Place them in a warm, dark place such as an enclosed propogating frame or an airing cupboard for about four to five days and do not disturb them. Then bring them out into the light and keep them at a temperature of 10°-13°C (50°-55°F) to flower. If you wish, the plants can be separated into single

10°C / 50°F

The bulbs should be kept at the lowest temperature indicated when planted.

15 – 21°C / 60–70°F

When in full bloom, the highest temperature indicated is required.

pots. The whole process from planting to flowering only takes three weeks. The bulbs can be replanted in October. Propagation can also be carried out in early autumn – just cover the crowns with soil.

CROCUS

Seeing a bowl of beautiful, yellow crocus flowering in mid winter can persuade anyone that spring is just about the corner. Crocuses are also available in other colours including: purple, violet and blue. Some are very delicately veined with purple and white; others have bright orange stamens.

The best type to gently force are the Dutch varieties. The prettiest crocuses are the ones that bloom in mid to late winter; these are members of the *Crocus chrysanthus* group. The autumn-flowering species such as *Crocus speciosus* and *C. sativus* are also worth considering.

Crocuses are grown in a gritty compost about 5cm (2in) deep, and spaced 2.5cm (1in) apart. They should be planted in the early autumn – except for the ones which flower in the autumn, pot these in mid summer. Ones which are going to be forced should be put outside in a cool place in the soil, covered up. Bring them in at the start of the winter and slowly give them more light and heat. Do not do it too quickly or you will end up with plenty of leaves but no flower. A final temperature of about 17°C (63°F) is recommended.

When the crocuses have finished flowering, keep feeding and watering them until the leaves wither and die naturally; then plant them out in the garden until the following autumn.

Popular crocus varieties: Blue pearl   Cream beauty

DAHLIA**

The small-growing dahlias are suitable for growing in containers. They are all half-hardy perennials. The miniature and dwarf ones include the cactus-flowered, pompon, decorative dahlias called Lilliput dahlias. They grow to about 45-60cm (1½-2ft).

These plants generally flower in the summer and in many lovely colours. They will normally bloom continuously, provided they are watered and fed adequately and that dead flowers are removed when the plants have finished flowering. The tubers can be stored away in boxes of peat and used again the following year.

ERANTHIS*

(Winter aconite)

Eranthis is a member of the buttercup family and is a very easy to grow tuber plant. It has bright, golden, star-shaped flowers surrounded by leafy bracts rather like a ruff. The plants bloom in early winter and can be placed in pots, tubs or window boxes. The tubers should be set about 5cm (2in) deep and the soil moistened afterwards.

Eranthis hyemalis is one of the easiest species to grow and when left to its own resources spreads through self-set seedlings. It grows to about 5-10cm (2-4in) tall. *E. tubergenii* has larger and brighter gold flowers on stems which are 7.5-12.5cm (3-5in) tall, but it is sterile.

Guinea Gold has particularly dark yellow flowers and foliage tinted with bronze.

C. biflorus   C. tomasinianus

GALANTHUS*
(Snow drop)

Snow drops are very hardy, pretty little plants which have single or double white flowers. The oval leaves grow very close to the plant. They can be potted in September or October about 5-5cm (2-3in) deep. As usual, they should be placed in a cool, dark place with a temperature of about 5°-7°C (40°-45°F). Keep the soil moist and when the tips appear move into more light and a temperature of about 10°C (50°F). When buds appear, keep in a temperature of about 16°C (60°F) until flowering occurs. The plants are quite happy without sun and bloom as early as January. When flowering has ceased the plants can be placed in the garden.

Some very attractive species of this plant are *G. elwesii,* which flowers in mid-winter, *G. nivalis,* which is a shorter and smaller species with double flowers, and *G. buvakus regubae-olgae* from Greece which flowers from early Autumn on.

HIPPEASTRUM**
(Amaryllis)

The most popular species, *Hippeastrum equestre,* comes from South America and the West Indies where it blooms in the winter or spring months with a bright green and red trumpet-shaped flower. Hybrids of this species are 'Apple Blossom', white and delicate pink in colour; 'Belinda', dark red in colour and 'Hecuba,' which is salmon.

These hybrids have large flowers which are about 10-12cm (1-2ft) tall; a few have a pleasant fragrance. The plant can be treated as an evergreen rather than letting it dry off during the summer months.

Hippeastrums have very large bulbs, about 10cm (4in) across and about 15cm (6in) long and they should be potted in 15cm (6in) pots containing a peaty compost with half the bulb protruding above the surface.

The bulbs should be planted in early to mid winter although specially prepared bulbs for early flowering will be available much earlier. Many hippeastrums are sold in kit form and are becoming very popular as gifts. When the bulbs have been planted, water them well and then stand them near warmth, the temperature should be at least 21°C (70°F). Water carefully until the leaves and flowerbud appear. Increase watering and move to a light place. Flowering occurs in eight weeks.

After flowering remove the flowerhead, feed with a potash-high feed until the leaves die down; continue watering and keep the plant in a sunny place. Give less water and feed less in late summer to make the plant dry up and take an enforced rest from about mid autumn to the beginning of February.

HYACINTHUS*
(Hyacinth)
The Dutch hyacinths, which have many hybrids, are really beautiful and difficult to compete with. They have fragrant, flowering spikes clustered with flowers. Blue, pink, purple, blue and white are just some of the colours available.

When grown in containers, hyacinths need standard potting compost, a lot of light and cool, humid conditions. They need watering when flowering and feeding until the leaves die down.

For early and mid winter flowering pot them in late summer, water well and put in a cool, dark place with a temperature of about 4°C (40°F) wrapped in black polythene for about 10 weeks; water occasionally if necessary. When there is a shoot 2.5cm (1-2in) tall bring the pot into a little light and warmth, gradually increase once the flower bud appears.

IRIS RETICULATA*
This species is a miniature purple iris which only grows to about 15cm (6in) tall. Plant the bulbs in late summer.

They flower in mid winter and should be planted in late summer in pans or small troughs. Insert them about 3.5cm (1½in) deep in a standard compost with some coarse sand for drainage. Put them outside in a shady place until mid autumn and then bring them inside again. Keep them cool, about 7°C (45°F) and, when the leaves begin to appear, give as much light as possible.

After flowering, remove the flowerheads but continue to water and feed until the leaves die naturally. Then dry the bulbs off and put in a warm place to ripen, outdoors if possible.

Hyacinths and crocuses can be grown in bulb glasses

LILIUM*
(Lily)

Hybrid lilies, which were introduced not so long ago, make very good houseplants and bloom in late winter. The treated bulbs are available in the shops in December and should be planted straight away in equal parts of leaf mould, loam and coarse sand plus some crushed charcoal. Plant three bulbs into a 15cm (6in) pot and cover with 5-7.5cm (2-3in) of soil. Keep the bulbs in the light and at a temperature of about 20°C (68°F). Popular varieties include: 'Brandywine', apricot-yellow; 'Cinnabar', maroon red; 'Enchantment', cherry-red; 'Paprika', deep crimson and 'Prosperity', lemon yellow.

Other lilies make ideal pot plants for flowering in the summer. *Lilium regale* and the hybrids, *L. longiflorum* and *L. auratum* are especially good. All should be planted in a rich soil mix of equal parts of loam, peat, leaf mould, well-decayed cow manure and some coarse sand for drainage. Again, use 15cm (6in) pots and cover the bulbs with 4cm (1½in) of soil. Place in a cool place and keep them away from sun until the buds sprout, when they can be brought into a warm room to flower.

MUSCARI*
(Grape hyacinth)

Grape hyacinths were once known as starch lilies because the bulb sap that they emit can be used for starching linen.

The easiest species to grow indoors are *Muscari botryoides* 'Album' which has white, grape-like flowers growing in cones on 15-25cm (6-10in) stems and *M. armeniacum* with its lovely, blue fragrant flowers and 'Blue Spire' which is a double blue cultivar.

Plant them in late autumn, early winter in 2.5cm (1in) of good soil mix and place in a cool place at a temperature of about 4.4°C (40°F) for six to eight weeks. Then put them in higher temperatures of about 10°-13°C (50°-55°F) so that they can bloom. They flower from late winter to early spring and make a very striking display when planted with daffodils, early tulips or primroses.

NARCISSUS*
(Daffodil, narcissi)

Daffodils and narcissi bloom in winter or early spring. They are hardy bulbs which grow very well indoors in pots or troughs.

Plant the bulbs in pots with their points upwards, but in troughs, bury them. The container should be at least 12.5cm (5in) deep if you want the bulbs to flower again next year. A normal potting compost should be used; five bulbs can be fitted in a 12.5cm (5in) wide pot or they should be placed 4cm

Tulips and grape hyacinths feature in
this display.

(1½in) apart in a trough or other container. Place the
container in a cool, dark place for ten weeks covered in black
polythene; keep the bulbs moist.

When the shoots are about 2.5cm (1in) high bring them into
a little light and warmth – at a temperature of 10°C (50°F).
When flower buds appear, give more light and warmth.
Prepared bulbs can be planted in mid-autumn for flowering in
early winter.

TULIPA*
(Tulip)
Tulips make lovely pot plants. Unprepared bulbs should be
planted in early September to mid October in good potting
mix and kept at temperatures of around 9°C (48°F) for 10 to 12
weeks, in a dark place. They should then be placed in warm
darkness at about 15.6°C (60°F) for two or three further weeks,
then put into a light living room to flower.

Specially prepared bulbs for flowering at Christmas should
be planted before the middle of September. Keep them cool
and in the dark as previously until the first week in December,
then place them in a temperature of 18°C (65°F) until growth
appears, at which point move them into the light to flower.
Good forcing varieties are 'Belgona', golden yellow; 'Brilliant
Star', scarlet and 'Doctor Plesman', orange red.

CACTI AND SUCCULENTS

Cacti and succulents are often considered to be rather dull, insignificant plants. This is, in fact, far from true. Many cacti have beautiful leaves and produce brilliant flowers in exotic colours, perhaps for weeks on end, or twice a year. The succulents can be distinguished by their fleshy leaves, which store moisture.

The best way to grow healthy plants is to recreate their normal habitats and give them heat, plenty of light, a dry atmosphere, occasional heavy watering and a drained potting mix.

Cacti are grown for their flowers and unusual shapes, succulents for their leaves. The cacti have pretty, often stemless, flowers in all colours except blue and succulents have highly ornamental leaves.

AGAVE*

The agaves are succulents which grow wild in Mexico and parts of America. The *Agave americana* grows in southern Europe and has thick, leathery leaves that form a sort of rosette, from the centre of which emerges the flower stem. The flowers take a long time to bloom and are not very interesting when they do.

In its natural habitat the plant's flower stem can grow as high as 7.5m (25ft) but for cultivation as a houseplant *Agave victoriae-reginae* is one which does not grow too big. The rosette takes many years to become fully grown – about 60cm (2ft) wide. The leaves are dark green in colour with white borders and thick and fleshy.

Temperatures should not fall below about 10°C (50°) in winter. Offsets can be taken in summer and planted singly in pots.

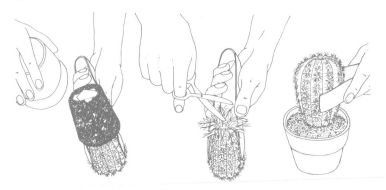

Handle prickly cactus with tongs when repotting; also remove dead roots

ALOE*

Aloe variegata is the most popular of the species, it originates from South Africa and is known as the Partridge-breasted aloe. It has dark green leaves which are variegated with white bands. The plant is about 10cm (4in) wide and very attractive. It flowers in the spring with light red, tubular flowers which grow on a 30cm (1ft) tall spike. This plant is ideal for cultivation in the home. Plenty of shade is preferred and it should be kept quite dry during the winter months. *A. jacunda* is a dwarf plant which grows very profusely. Do not let the temperature fall below 5°C (41°F).

ASTROPHYTUM*

Bishop's cap cactus or Star or Sea-urchin cactus. The most easy species to grow is *Astrophytum myriostigma* (Bishop's cap cactus). When a young plant it has an almost circular body covered with white scales. It produces small, fragrant yellow flowers in the summer. *A. asterias* (Star or Sea-urchin cactus) resembles a flattened ball, with eight ribs and pale yellow flowers which are 2.5cm (1in) wide. The plant grows to about 4cm (1½in) high and about 10cm (4in) wide when cultivated in pots. However, in the wild it can grow to as much as 20cm (8in) in width.

The ideal minimum temperature for Astrophytum is about 5°C (41°F).

Cacti, of varying shapes.

COTYLEDON**

Cotyledon undulata is one of the most popular of this species
and is a very attractive plant. The light green leaves have a
touch of silvery white and tend to curl. The plant grows to
about 45cm (1½ft). The flowers, which appear in the summer,
are pale yellow and red and bell-shaped. The plant will benefit
from some shade in the summer but a good deal of light in the
winter months. Moderate watering is needed all the year
round; never water or spray overhead as this can spoil the
leaves. The minimum temperature should be about 7°C (45°F).

CRASSULA*

Crassulas are succulents that originate mainly from South
Africa. They can either be shrubby or herbaceous and have
pointed, rounded or prickly leaves.

   Crassula arborescens is a small bushy plant which grows
slowly and reaches 90-120cm (3-4ft) only after many years. It

Succulents provide colourful arrangements when planted together.

has thick, shiny oval leaves and white starry flowers in late
spring and early summer. *C. lycopodioides* is also widely
grown and has small leaves which are pressed against the
stems in layers.

Crassulas generally are easy to grow but they must be
regularly watered or the leaves will shrivel and the plants will
never bloom. In the rest period after flowering and growing,
very little water is needed.

EUPHORBIA**
(Crown of thorns)

Euphorbia milii, (Crown of thorns) is a succulent with thick,
fleshy stems, a tough, greyish skin and spines which protrude
menacingly from the stems. The prickles are however, hidden
by rounded, green leaves and small, bright red flowers. This
lovely little plant will flower nearly all year round with the
right treatment; it comes from Madagascar and needs a warm
sunny place with no humidity all year round. Temperatures
should never fall below 10°C (50°F) or the leaves will drop off
and the stems will shrivel.

Water only a little in winter; too much moisture will cause
the leaves to fall. A standard potting compost should be used
and the plant needs to be fed occasionally in summer.

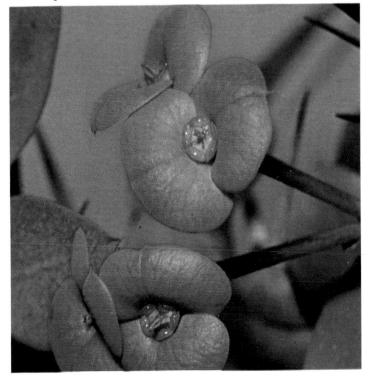

Red flowers of Crown of thorns

GYMNOCALYCIUM*

Not a particularly noticeable cacti, gymnocalyciums have spiny globes about 5-15cm (2-6in) in diameter and flower from late spring to mid-summer, depending on the species. The colours are pink, red and sometimes yellow or white; the blooms are large and last for four to five days. They do not need as much light as other cacti; in winter keep them moist and do not allow them to dry out.

Some gymnocalyciums have virtually no chlorophyll. An extraordinary-looking cactus is the cultivar 'Red Bull' which has a bright red ball growing on top of a prickly green base. It has been grafted onto a stock of *Myrtillocactus* to keep it without chlorophyll. It is grown for its red colour but hardly ever flowers – another variety is bright yellow – and 'Hiboran Nishiki' has green and red stripes; all come from Japan.

KALANCHOE*

Kalanchoes are part of the Crassula family and are also succulents. The most commonly grown houseplant is *Kalanchoe blossfeldiana;* it flowers in the winter with tiny, red clusters which last for at least several weeks. Cut back after flowering to just a pair of leaves – these are rounded, shiny and green. Other varieties with yellow and pink flowers have been developed as this plant is so easy to grow.

It is a plant which is used to a short day so its flowering period can be changed by shortening the day length in spring and summer. After winter flowering, give less water until new shoots and leaves appear then increase it and give as much

Rebutia (p. 90)

light as possible in early and mid summer. This will help to ripen the growth for flowering the following winter. A minimum temperature of 10°C (50°F) is needed in winter; temperatures in summer are normal. Some humidity and light is necessary. Feed from time to time in winter and make sure it does not dry out in summer; Kalanchoes do need more food than most succulents. Repot in spring or autumn in standard potting compost.

OPUNTIA*
(Prickly pear, Bunny ears)
There are many different species of opuntia – native of North, South and Central America. The most well-known type consists of long, joined 'pads' which look like ears – hence one of the common names. Some are smooth, others are hairy and some have spines. The flowers are big and showy in many colours including: red, purple, yellow, pink and white. They do not often bloom as houseplants as they have to grow quite big before they flower.

Opuntia microdasys albispina is good in the home. It is a small, compact plant with hairy pads and can produce pale-yellow flowers if well treated. *O. ficus-indica* (Fruiting fig) grows into a bushy plant about 1m (3ft) tall and is also grown for its fruit which appears after the yellow flowers.

The fruits of the opuntia can be eaten, and are grown in America for canning, although they can be eaten fresh.

Opuntia

REBUTIA*

Rebutias are named after P. Rebut, a French cactus grower of the nineteenth century. The plants originate from northern Argentina and Bolivia and often grow high up in the mountains at altitudes of 3600m (11,000ft). They seem to need very little nourishment yet flower abundantly – some flower twice a year. They are easy to grow and good plants for the home, especially in a sunny position. The plants are rounded in shape and many offsets can be taken so that you can have a container full of plants, which, in summer, each produce funnel-shaped flowers coloured orange, yellow, red, pink, salmon or white. Sometimes, small red fruits are also produced.

Gritty compost and a pan container rather than a pot are best for this cactus. Water well in summer when it is growing but keep virtually dry in winter. Take care when changing the watering from summer to winter. A lot of sun and some humidity is also necessary in summer. Keep on the cool side in winter, about 7°C (45°F) until early spring. Increase the plant by taking offsets when you repot in spring or summer. Rotting can occur if the compost is too wet or warm in winter. Beware of red spider mites and mealy bugs which can attack in summer.

RHIPSALIDOPSIS GAERTNERI*

(Easter cactus)

This is a leaf cactus, an epiphyte – a plant which grows on trees and in tree forks. The Easter cactus differs from the Christmas cactus in that it flowers in the spring, has much more prominent petals and the stamens are enclosed within the flowers rather than growing out of them. It also has pointed notches rather than the blunt ones of the Christmas cactus. So you should easily be able to tell the variety apart. It is also cared for very differently.

The cactus rests from late autumn to early winter, but from that time it should be watered more often with soft water. Flowerbuds for the red flowers start to peep through in late winter and this is when feeding, too, should start again and the temperature should be slowly increased to 16°-18°C (60°-65°F). When the plant has finished flowering, repot into peaty, acid compost and place outside when all risk of frost has passed, or in a cool place with some shade. Do not let it dry out during this growing period. Bring indoors in the autumn and keep at a temperature of about 10°C (50°F); water sufficiently to keep the compost moist. Keep away from artificial light in autumn and early winter as this can disturb the blooming.

This plant, due to indecision as to which genus it belongs to, is sometimes sold as *Schlumbergera, Zygocactus* or *Epiphylum.*

Rhipsalidopsis gaertneri

SCHLUMBERGERA BUCKLEYI**
(Christmas cactus)
Just to be confusing, this plant is sometimes sold under the
name *Zygocactus truncatus* but it is certainly the Christmas
cactus. This leafy cactus is an epiphyte from the rain forests of
Brazil, where it actually grows on trees. It therefore likes a
humus compost containing peat or sphagnum moss.

It has fuchsia-like pink flowers which bloom in late autumn
until mid winter. The buds appear from the last pad in the
chain that makes up the stem. The more stems on the plant the
better as only one flower is produced by each stem. A mature
plant can be about 45cm (1½ft) wide with lots of stems; the
highest it will grow however, is about 23cm (9in).

When it is flowering, water well as for any other houseplant,
give plenty of light, a temperature of about 13°-18°C
(55°C-65°F) and some humidity. Buds will be lost if the plant is
moved, the temperature or the light is changed, it is short of
water or in a draught, or if it is subjected to gas or a dry
atmosphere. As you can gather the plant is sensitive at this
time!

When flowering has finished slow down the watering.

BROMELIADS

Bromeliads are very striking, tropical plants which come from the South and Central American jungles, where they grow on the trees. They have rosettes of stiff, leathery, strap-like leaves which spray out from a central crown. A tube in the central crown collects rainwater and it is from here that the stems and flowers grow. Once the plants have flowers they eventually die but the leaves will remain attractive for several months.

Good light, but not direct sunlight, is normally preferred, humidity is not essential; the atmosphere does not have to be too warm but ensure that the compost is moist at all times. Also, regularly check the rain-water level in the central funnel and feed through this, especially in the growing season. The only pests that seem to attack are scale insects and mealy bugs.

AECHMEA*
(Urn plant)

Aechmea fascinata (syn. *A. rhodocyanea, Billbergia rhodocyanea*) is one of the most ornamental plants and one of the easiest to grow. It is a lovely, long-lasting plant, with grey-green leaves banded with white, and bright blue flowers which last for about four months. In good growing conditions small berries form after the flowers but it is unlikely in those that are houseplants. The leaves are a bit spiny at the sides and have channels to collect rainwater for the central funnel.

Aechmeas like average summer temperatures, about 21°C (70°F), and good light – including sun, but not the midday sun. In winter the minimum temperature should be 7°C (45°F).

Always make sure the water in the central funnel is topped

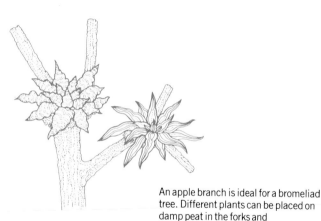

An apple branch is ideal for a bromeliad tree. Different plants can be placed on damp peat in the forks and inconspicuously wired to the branches.

up with tepid, soft water during the spring, summer and early autumn and occasionally feed through the funnel. Also keep the compost slightly moist; water less in winter.

BILLBERGIA NUTANS*
(Angel's tears)
    The plant has long, leathery narrow leaves which resemble grass and grow in funnel-shaped clusters 30-45cm (1-1½ft) tall and wide. The flowers are very attractive; they hang from the 25cm (10in) stems and are rose-pink coloured bracts from which grow long flowers coloured navy blue, yellow, green and pink, all together. Flowering starts in the spring.
    A peaty compost is needed for the plant, which also likes shade – too much light makes the leaves go a yellowish-green colour. Average warmth in summer is necessary with a minimum winter temperature of 7°C (45°F), plus normal bromeliad watering and feeding.

CRYPTANTHUS*
(Earth star)
Cryptanthuses are grown as houseplants for their decorative leaves which are green, variegated in cream, yellow, wine pink and other colours.
    Cryptanthus bivittatus is the one most commonly grown. This small plant is only about 15-20cm (6-8in) wide and it does not grow very high. There are wide cream stripes down the leaves which turn pink in bright light.
    All the plants like a peaty compost and adequate watering and feeding via the centre. The temperature should not fall below 8°-9°C (46°-48°F) in the winter.

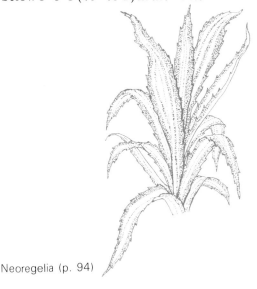

Neoregelia (p. 94)

GUZMANIA*

Guzmanias, especially the hybrid varieties, have been very popular as houseplants over the last 10 to 15 years. The flowerhead resembles a spear in shape, although in some species it slowly opens out to resemble a waterlily. *Guzmania lingulata* grows to a height of 30cm (1ft) and has a bright red flowerhead and small white flowers surrounded by orange and yellow bracts. *G. zahnil* has olive green leaves and red bracts on the flower stem. The flowerhead is yellow with white flowers. It grows to about 60cm (2ft). *G. berteroniana* has a lovely, red flowerhead and yellow flowers. The leaves are light green or deep red and it reaches a height of around 45cm (1½ft).

All the species flower in the winter and need a minimum temperature of 16°C (60°F).

NEOREGELIA**

These bromeliads differ from other species in that the flowers never completely emerge from the central funnel. They flower in late spring and early summer, blooms forming over the top. All species have handsome leaves which can be either plain or variegated. *Neoregelia carolinae* 'Tricolor' is a striking plant which is easy to obtain. It has dark green, leathery leaves with central yellow stripes. The funnel, however, is bright red the colour flushing along the leaves and gradually fading towards the middle of each, and the central flowerhead is red with violet flowers.

N. concentrica is also popular. It has 30cm (12in) long leaves which are green on one side and banded dark grey on the other. The inner leaves are purple and the flowers are purple to blue.

General care for these plants is that normal for bromeliads but in winter they need a higher temperature of about 13°C (55°F), and about 21°C (70°F) in the summer, plus a great deal of light.

TILLANDSIA*

There are many different varieties of Tillandsia. It is found both in tropical rainforests and deserts, and there are therefore terrestrial and epiphytic forms, requiring appropriate care and attention.

Spanish moss is an epiphytic species. A bromeliad tree is ideal for growing this plant so that the long trails can hang down from the branches. *T. lindeniana* has large, brilliant blue flowers emerging from a flattened spike of deep rose-pink bracts on a stem about 30cm (1ft) long. It is a showy plant, flowering in summer. The leaves are narrow and pointed in dark green and purple, altogether making a very spectacular plant.

VRIESEA**

(Flowering sword)

Vrieseas are named after the nineteenth-century Dutch botanist, W.H. de Vriese and are native to the Central and South American rain forests. Flowerheads can be red, yellow or red and yellow together.

Vriesea splendens (Flaming sword) has leaves 50cm (20in) long, striped in dark brown-purple. The flowerhead, which is shaped like a sword, is red with yellow flowers. It blooms in mid to late summer and the flowers may last for two months. The leaves will remain attractive for some time after that. *V. gigantea* (Syn. *V. tessellata)* is another good species and it has 45cm (1½ft) leaves with yellow markings on top and red-purple markings beneath; however, it rarely flowers as a houseplant.

Vriseas need normal treatment for light and feeding but the winter temperature must not fall below 18°C (65°F). Water moderately in summer with tepid soft water, but in winter empty most of the water from the funnel as the plants will get enough moisture from humidity.

Neoregelia carolinae 'Tricolor'.

INDEX